PRAYER
Woman

VICTORIOUS WARRIOR

ABIDING ON THE VINE

TO POUR OUT

THE PRESENCE OF GOD

OVER HER HUSBAND

41 DAY DEVOTIONAL & FAST

BY

LAURA GANT

WATER the WELL

Scripture quotations are taken from
English Standard Version 2016.
Used by permission. All rights reserved.

Published on 2/22/2022
2023 Revised & Expanded Edition Published by Water The Well, Inc.

Printed in the United States of America
Library of Congress Cataloging-in-Publication Data
1 3 2 3 0 1 6 5 3 9 1

PRAYER WOMAN: VICTORIOUS WARRIOR ABIDING ON THE VINE TO
POUR OUT THE PRESENCE OF GOD OVER HER HUSBAND

Written by Laura Gant
ISBN: 9798985336924 (paperback)
Hardback and ebook: DISCONTINUED

More written by Laura Gant:
*Found In The River: A Journey Through Loss, Transformation &
Healing By The Power of God*
ISBN: 9798985336948

A 41-DAY JOURNAL
OF FASTING & PRAYER
WITH JESUS
ON BEHALF OF
YOUR HEART & THE HEART OF YOUR

Husband

COMPLETE YOUR 41 DAYS IN THIS JOURNAL

WITH ITS COMPANION

AUDIO & VIDEO SERIES

BY USING THE

DAILY QR CODES.

SCAN AND REGISTER FOR ACCESS

DEDICATION

To my Great Abba, Jesus,
The reason for prayer,
Lord of my life.
I am nothing without YOU.

To everyone woman
who has covered me in Scripture
and been my friend in the fire.

This book is dedicated to all the wives
who seek God's best for their husbands through
their prayerful support as his helpmate.

To the love of my life
who is my dearest, treasure of gold
on this side of Heaven;
my miracle,
my answered prayer,
my covenant partner,
my truest friend,
my beloved husband,
my dream,
my forever home.
Cary, I am honored to be the loudest woman alive
to proclaim your highest praises,
and believe for you to live as an
Ephesians 5 husband to me and a man
after God's heart.

INTRODUCTION

Hello Warrior Queen!

Yes, you! Father God holds your full potential for power.

You are fashioned with great purpose in your Godly position as wife.

You are a Warrior Queen getting ready to put on her Prayer Mantle as the wife in her home. From one wife to another, the divine position we have been placed in, is that which is given from Jesus to us. Once we adopt the fullness of what this means, we will forever be changed.

Over the course of the next 41 days, you and I, arms linked, will traverse through areas of pain & wilderness to springs of healing. We will dig our trenches, bust down locked doors of the heart, and climb those mountains. This prayer journal is your call to rise from pain to power. Out of the ashes, will come beauty. Declare it! Jesus will become your everything. It's time live like it!

I encourage you to fast during these forty-one days, as we immerse ourselves into Scripture and prayer, and learn to be still in God's presence. Don't over-think, adopt His Truth, open your heart, your hands, and your mind to how God has been out in front, sifting, shifting, clearing, and moving for your good. Perhaps you have started this book because you are in search for healing in your heart or more unity in your marriage. Perhaps you are longing for a deeper prayer life, or to have daily direction to grow in the Word and prayer. Or perhaps, you are faced with a broken circumstance and you need answers.

Woman, oh lovely and dearest daughter of God,

YOU ARE IN THE RIGHT PLACE:

Prayer changes everything. Jesus is the Way!

Laura

PRAYER*Woman*

41 DAYS OF UNITY

PURPOSE OF PRAYER

Are you searching for a move of God in your life and in your marriage? How do you know that God hears you when you pray? Have you been crying out for a shift? Woman, as you rise up in the power of prayer, you move the heart of God, who in turn, begins to move in your life and in your spouse.

Are you ready for prayer and fasting to change everything in your life? I have witnessed impossible things become possible. I have been the recipient of bold prayers that only were answered because of Jesus. When you are rooted in Him, your identity in Him takes precedence over every circumstance. Here, is where you embark on a journey of developing unshakable faith in Him, because He holds your position and there is nothing mankind can do to remove you from being His child. You were formed in your mother's womb and you were known before the beginning of the Garden. You are fully loved and known by your Creator, and Jesus will never stop pursuing you with His kindness.

Psalm 139:1 "O Lord, you have searched me and known me!"

Psalm 139:13,14 "For you formed my inward parts; you knitted me together in my mother's womb. I praise you, for I am fearfully and wonderfully made. Wonderful are your works; my soul knows it very well."

When we are known by the King of Heaven, we find that our position for everything else flows out from it. Your various trials in this world and in this flesh, your dealings of human nature; it's all so fragile and temporary, and therefore, imperative that each moment counts for eternity. God has etched eternity into us from the very beginning. Eccl. 3:11 "He has made everything beautiful in its time." Eccl. 3:20-22 "All go to one place. All are from the dust, and to dust all return. Who knows whether the spirit of man goes upward and the spirit of the beast goes down into the earth? So I saw that there is nothing better than that a man should rejoice in his work, for that is his lot."

When Eternity is so deeply etched upon our souls, it changes everything about us. Our commitment strengthens to show up to every minute as the transformed daughter. Our behavior, attitude, motive, and intentions become pure in His presence. God's power compels and moves us into a space so pure - no fragmented view of life can live here. His glory dwells in this place where the Prayer Woman lingers for a drink. As you parter with His promises, His Way, and His Truth, experience Him shift and remake every part of you, from the inside-out.

Heaven is calling you by your new name. We don't know the time-frame of being here on earth. Father is calling His bride to live a surrendered life; a life laid down. We must be compelled to live with eternity in focus and reconciled to our true identity in Christ, as this side of Heaven is so temporary. Health can be snatched from us in a moment. The reality has become increasingly vivid the more I have pressed into His presence. His will, His love, and His vision for our existence must radically shift our awareness and urgency of time. It's time to live wide awake to His will for our marriage.

Being slow to speak, seeking kindness, showing more grace, being more loving, allowing more of Jesus and less of me, being more intentional in being like Jesus inside my relationships....these of of great importance. These places must flow from a saturated well of faith, hope, and love in Father.

When we can get a grip on our true identity in Christ, suddenly the veil on our eyes falls and we can see how everything in Him is possible. His Love conquers fear, so there is nothing to fear in overcoming self in order to carry out the purpose of God, and to truly be on fire in the full power of Him who came to save us.

This Truth is compelling and literally has the power to shake off every fear that is gripping your life. Will you accept the challenge to align yourself with it?

The fears of: 'I can't', 'I don't know how', 'I want to but', 'sounds good but I can deal with where I am'...These all stem from you placing yourself as the god of your own life instead of Jesus being the King and Lord of your life. We can no longer say "I trust you, Jesus, and I'm a Christian and believe that you're my God", and simultaneously say "but it's too hard, I'm in pain, I am stuck."

Inside your personal journey with Jesus, there is a grand and fulfilling identity provided to you by the King Himself. In this identity, you no longer lead your situations from 'ME or I'. Saying yes to Jesus means He becomes your Leader, your Shepherd. All things must begin and end with Jesus, not self.

Pray with me:
"Thank you, Abba, for breathing life inside my lungs. I know that in You, everything and anything can change in a moment. I need this urgency in my life."

"I acknowledge the resources You are giving me and I praise You for being my answer. Thank you for giving me another day to honor you. Thank you for setting eternity within me so that all I desire is Your real fruit. Show me how to sow the fruit of the Holy Spirit by spending time seeking Your face. Come unlock Your storehouses for freedom, forgiveness, reconciliation, restitution, purity, unity, peace, salvation, revival, unconditional love, grace, and kindness. Show up victoriously for my marriage. Vengeance is the Lord's not mine. I release control for how I want this to go. Instead, I choose to abide in Love, and run to the well of living water, where I walk daily as a well watered woman in Jesus. Amen."

Prayer Woman, set a Living Aura® to: set the captives free, enable peace, bring joy, stir up unity, deliver and make whole. Emit great courage and strength because you are connected to the Source. Be faithful to your marriage covenant, run the race of faith with endurance, and break the chains of sin through your obedience to God. Plant good seed in fertile soil. Reap a harvest of spiritual fruit.

God will move the immovable, and provide your miracle despite the wilderness...it's who JESUS is, working alive within you. Stay hidden under the shadow of His wings. To step out from underneath His shelter, is to relinquish and abandon the protection of His overcoming power meant for your good. Decide today, to ask for wisdom and knowlege of the will of God. This journey will guide you out of your old ways the closer you get to Jesus: out of sadness, through the pain and suffering, and into hope. It's easy to entertain grief and sadness when you have been unfairly treated, but it is **what** you decide to do with it that makes all of the difference.

Are you needing a miracle in your marriage?

Are you ready to stop coming up short as a Godly wife?

Are you ready to say YES to Unity?

Are you ready to watch giants fall?

Are you ready to witness your husband's victories?

Are you ready to laugh without fear of the future?

Are you ready to unleash the queen within you?

Much love and prayer over you,

LAURA GANT

YOU ARE INVITED TO JOIN A

movement

OF WOMEN ON FIRE FOR JESUS

TAKE THIS GROWTH FURTHER

THAN THIS JOURNAL

& JOIN OUR DISCIPLESHIP COMMUNITY AT

WWW.LAURAGANT.COM

PRAISE FOR PRAYER WOMAN

"Your book has been so powerful. When you have that joy inside, there is no better feeling. Nothing can compare to the joy He can give you. When you experience that, you crave it more and more."
- Tarryn R.

"I loved reading this prayer journal. I've already done it twice! I saw God work so much in my marriage during this time. Sometimes I would see the prayer answered almost immediately within my husband. So many little miracles. I also loved the mindset shifts I had about my marriage that helped equip me for more constructive ways to approach situations. Thank you, Laura, for being obedient in writing this." - **Natalie L.**

"Empty to full. This book is a source of HOPE. It is written with her desire for us to be blessed and filled! Each chapter is concise to read in a few minutes with space to practice writing out a sincere prayer, thoughts of gratitude, or empty out what we carry deep in the heart. It's therapeutic and beneficial for our mind and soul, like exercising our brain and body with careful guidance. It is a wonderful resource of encouragement and opportunity for growth!" - **Molly G.**

"God never stops talking to you through Laura. I am in complete amazement over the way that God has spoken directly to me, each and every day through the words given to Laura. I have had so many revelations and breakthroughs as I journaled over the word each and every day. I went into his journey thinking it would be about my husband; while, yes, there's powerful prayers to speak over him, it has been more a softening of my heart that has left me to a deeper surrender. I will be doing this one on repeat! Every word was on point and right on time." - **Joni K.**

FORWARD BY NALONI LEE

Hi sweet, beloved sister!

I have known Laura Gant since we were toddlers. We never lost touch and have always had that 'best friends' of the heart type of friendship! In the last few years, it has grown deeper into a spiritual sisterhood unlike any other. We have both given our all to our Abba Father as His daughters, for His Kingdom and glory, and are ever inspiring, encouraging, and speaking life into one another.

I have had the privilege of journeying with Laura as she dated, married, and was divorced from her first husband, walked into her journey of healing, and known now in her second and final marriage, which Abba has been preparing for her for a very long time! I love to recall back to when she told me about this man she had met who loved the Lord and the way the Holy Spirit confirmed their union with His presence. I was overjoyed, teary-eyed and rejoicing in gratitude to see the faithfulness of God that I had dreamed of for her!

It's one thing to fight for your husband in prayer, but another to watch a sister do the same thing alongside you. What a joy it has been to be able to encourage and inspire her too. Before she dove into writing this book, Holy Spirit was fully alive in her. Laura shared with me what she was about to do. I felt aglow in gratitude for seeing Abba moving not only in, but through her life! This is a woman who has come through the fire, time and again, but ever-yielding to the work that Jesus is doing in her. Watching right before my eyes, the work of the Refiner's fire, as He stripped away all that isn't in alignment for His plan and ultimate dream for Laura's life, for her marriage and household. Yet it seems the more she walks through the valleys with Abba, the more she shines with His light. And it is so beautiful to behold!!

In the pages to follow, Laura addresses every angle and approach to this journey. Emotionally, mentally, spiritually, femininely, as is very needed because this mantle of being a Prayer Woman is a whole-being thing. It is not ever something to be taken lightly, ever again. You see, we have this GIFT! This incredible, blessed, wild adventure that we are called to as the warrior queen for our husbands, our marriages and our households!! Oh what an honor it is!!!!!

It's hard to grasp before we begin on this journey, the power we have as daughters of the King. I remember back to when I too felt powerless. I had lost myself in my marriage and had no idea that I could rise up from where I was in that time. I saw breakthrough and began to pursue Abba's heart with relentless abandon and passion, intentionally inviting Him into my marriage as an equal part and taking things to Him more than to my husband.

God restructured everything in me and taught me how to be the wife He has called me to be! I look back with nothing but an abundance of gratitude for all that He has renewed and revolutionized in me and in my marriage! As I read Laura's book, prior to printing, I am eating up every single sentence and excited to read it again after publication! (I have never read a book twice; this one I have no doubt I will!!). Although how can I say, Laura's book? This is God and Laura's book. As her boys have affectionately told her, "Mama, go work on God's book!" I am already seeing Proverbs 31:28, "Her children rise up and call her blessed; her husband also, and he praises her!" Laura and her husband do both praise one another! Why? Because the love of Abba has filled their wells and they respond to one another from His fullness now, not their lack! Think about that? How amazing is that?! Life-giving from all angles!

I cannot express how privileged I am to be on the front row of this book, and the years, journey, heartache, trials, wounds, stretching and growing that have preluded the victory in Jesus that I now see. I see His heart and love His work here to such a profound degree! Laura is and continues to be one the greatest blessings in my life. My dream and prayer now is that her voice and heart of blessing be magnified to an even greater extent! Through her book may you truly feel as she is offering her hand for you to grasp, so that you too can discover God's victory in your life, marriage and household! Will you, dear daughter of our King, accept her invitation and take a step into the sweet sanctuary Abba has been preparing for you? You need nothing more to qualify than a willing heart and yourself, just as you are now. Come with us, as we dive into these super nourishing pages together. Freely allow Abba to undo and redo it all, as He forms you into His Prayer Woman, a woman ever after His own heart!

Much love, Naloni Lee
P.S. I cannot wait to hear your story!!!!

DAY 1:
POWER OF IDENTITY & PRAYER

As the wife in your home and marriage, you carry the power of your PRAYER MANTLE!

The wife's mantle is her sovereignly, delegated role of assisting in her husband's calling. We are starting with this topic on Day 1 because knowing who you are in your position is the foundation.

YOU, my dear, are a woman of God, and as the appointed wife, you have the opportunity to step into the powerful responsibility and blessing of being the helper by activating your PRAYERS.

Your mantle carries the delegated authority and power to move your husband as you bring your prayers to JESUS! God is pleased by you coming to Him on behalf of your husband. The power of your mantle maximizes the life of your husband beyond your imagination. God listens to you, and goes to move beyond what you can comprehend for your husband's good. When you, as his wife, are aligned with taking everything to JESUS instead of him, you allow JESUS to carry the burden and unlock favor.

Your prayers are your secret weapon for your husband's good. If you need a move in your marriage, or if he needs a move in his life, then pray for his peace, pray for his safety, his courage, for his spirit to be receptive of Jesus' will, but ultimately, pray from a place of believing in his good.

When you go into your place of prayer, don't bring your wish list, your desires, your worries, your fears, your lack, your pain, or your inability to see God's big picture.

When you leave all of that at the feet of Jesus, He will be faithful to love on your soul and provide for your needs. I know that it might be hard to understand this, but God truly can fulfill your every need. He will likely do it in His own way and timing, which is much bigger and better than you can imagine right now. So take heart, daughter!

Placing your husband's good above your own is being intentional to prefer him over what you can see with the natural eye, or from a position of unfulfillment. This means, in God's presence, Jesus can remove the scales from your eyes, removing the 'self' filter and giving you the 'JESUS' filter. He shifts you from a narrow vision to a place where you can intercede and lavish faith over your husband.

Getting outside of yourself in this way, I've witnessed Jesus move instantly in my own life. It used to take many days for me to know that God had moved in my situation. Then, as I continued to mature in letting go of my control, God began to move within seconds from when I had begun to pray.

A wife who flourishes in her role is accountable to respectful behavior and responses to her husband. A wife's helping role can not afford to be forfeited by inappropriate behavior, failure to surrender control, nagging, lack of grace, complaining, bringing lack, teaching him like a child, and not believing in his good.

Lay it at Jesus' feet.

LISTEN & WATCH

Proverbs 18:10
The name of the Lord is my strong tower; I run to it and am safe.
Psalm 16:5
The Lord is my chosen portion and my cup; you hold my lot.
Psalm 46:10
I am here, being still, knowing that you are God. As for me, my heart will be still.
John 15:4
Abide in me, and I in you. As the branch cannot bear fruit by itself, unless it abides on the vine, neither can you, unless you abide in me.
Matthew 7:20
You will be recognized from your fruit.
Matthew 7:7
Ask, and it will be given to you; seek, and you will find; knock, and it will be opened to you. For anyone who asks receives, and the one who seeks finds, and to the one who knocks it will be opened.

PRAY: *SAFE IN FATHER'S ARMS*

I am safe in my Father's arms.

I rest in knowing that, here in the presence of the King,

I am held and I am known, and I am secure.

It is in this place from where

I move and align myself in love.

This is where I rise daily, and out of me

flows the riches of a spirit of faith and the real fruit of

abiding in God. This fruit is centered within me

and is securely sheltered, so that the only thing that

flows out of me to my Husband comes from safety in Jesus.

So, here I live and pray that I will no longer take back

the control of the safe space inside of me

because it belongs to God.

I am covered by this shelter, and

I extend this shelter over my

husband through my actions.

Father, help me submit all of my thoughts,

emotions, heart, motives, and actions so that

You can do what only You can do: give me rest.

God, You have my husband, not me.

I will not hold worry over him.

I will not hold fear and doubt and unforgiveness.

Give my husband safety in Your arms.

JOURNAL PROMPT

Write out a verse with your own prayer on safety.

DAY 2:
GRACE REWROTE MY STORY

Today, we meditate upon Grace: the story of how Jesus made you alive in Him, and brought you from death in sin, to life in Him through redemption. When Jesus died on the cross, He washed away your sins: past, present, and future. Knowing this, you now have the commission to live out this amazing transformation in your mind and spirit, and cultivate a newness into your marriage.

Grace writes the 'God story' of how He views you, and how you are to view his son, your husband. Through this lens we see purity. I call them "God Goggles". Seeing your husband as pure, in the light of Jesus, is an example of you marching on mission for your husband's good. Even if he cannot see it or walk it out for himself, your prayers and actions spiritually call him into it.

When we walk by the Spirit, the desires of the flesh begin to die. To ponder and linger upon both your spouse's fleshly mistakes, and even your own, is to pick up a battle that no longer exists. The battle of his spirit belongs to the Lord. It's already been won. The more swift you are to align yourself to what Jesus has done for your husband, the more apt you are to pray from a place of purity and integrity.

Your Godly role as wife requires you to renew your mind and spirit daily. Your spirit is the lamp of the Lord. It burns pure and bright when you allow Jesus to search your innermost parts. When this happens, you may even become very uncomfortable if you are holding on to anything that is not from God. If you are, they are things that come against your husband and the covenant God gave you for your marriage. You carry the authority of standing with the Truth of Jesus that set you free from sin. It is the wife's responsibility to view her husband through the eyes of Jesus. Pivot your understanding of sin: it's broken and conquered. Stop holding on to the pain that it causes. Forgive! Forgive even if it was never a sin against you personally; forgive because God forgives. Hold redemption as a banner over his head by praying blessing of faith from a place of joy.

It is imperative to relinquish your view of sin on his life by letting go of the lie that you need to remind him of his sin, and react from a place of captivity, as if it's the only way for him to become better; it's not. In other words, Grace rewrote his story, from death to life, so it is by his actions that he is redeemed (Ephesians 2:8); it is the gift of God.

As a wife who stands up for her husband's good, you must align yourself with this gift of God for him by agreeing that grace is sufficient for him; it is made perfect in his weakness (1 Corinthians 12:9).

As the wife, you can no longer hold a sin over your husband, because he is already forgiven and set free in Christ. How incredibly freeing this is! The bottom line for today's study is to view your husband through redemption's eyes so that your prayers call him forth into the fullness of his Godly potential.

LISTEN & WATCH

Romans 12:2
Be transformed by the renewal of my mind, that by testing I may discern what is the will of God, what is good and acceptable and perfect.

Psalm 51:10
Create in me a clean heart, O God, and renew a right spirit within me.

Romans 8:5b,6
Those who live according to the Spirit set their minds on the things of the Spirit. For to set the mind on the flesh is death, but to set the mind on the Spirit is life and peace.

Galatians 5:16,17
Walk by the Spirit, and you will not gratify the desires of the flesh. For the desires of the flesh are against the Spirit, and the desires of the Spirit are against the flesh...

Proverbs 20:27
The spirit of man is the lamp of the Lord, searching all his innermost parts.

PRAY: *HE IS ALIVE IN GRACE*

Father, my husband is the recipient of your grace:
your beautiful love story of how You came to rescue us all from
the clutches of sin so that we can live with you for eternity.
I am grateful that You chose my husband to live with eternity
in his heart. I praise You for setting him free from how sin
wanted to write his story.
Jesus, I pray that You will continue to keep him in Your hedge of
protection against the battles of flesh that want to
distract, destroy, and cause chaos.
My husband is redeemed, set free in the Spirit
as a redeemed son in Your Kingdom.
I align my heart to what You have done and commit to coming
to You in prayer from here and not from me.
Bless my husband with Your agape love.
Bless his actions, thoughts, words and deeds
to reflect the story You have written upon his heart.
I praise You for the sacrifice and resurrection
of Christ so that my husband has direct access to You at
all times for operating in Your victory.
Open his spiritual eyes to know and walk in this daily victory
so that he may overcome fear, old patterns, and walk as a
warrior of the fruit of the Spirit.

JOURNAL PROMPT

Write your prayer for your husband's grace story.

DAY 3:
JESUS IS THE WAY: BELIEVE FOR IT

Jesus is The Way when there seems to be no way. I love the power in CeCe Winan's song: *Believe For It*. Listen to this song as you begin to set the stage for today. I encourage you to be still in God's presence, worship, and allow the atmosphere around you to be filled with the Truth and Hope from Heaven.

What are you believing for in your home and marriage?
In what areas do you feel like you cannot believe?
When there seems to be no way, when you feel confined, the walls pressing closer in around you, cramped in a ball, no way out or through, will you choose to say "Jesus is the Way"?!

When you come before the King who holds the keys to your heart and the storehouses of Heaven, how can we skip over asking Jesus to give us a portion of faith for this day? Ask and you shall receive. Knock, and it will be opened. If you are not able to fully believe in faith for the breakthrough that you are fasting about, ask God. He will give it to you in His presence. Go into your prayer time already having this belief.

Prayer is where we come to be a woman, well watered from the living water found in His presence and Word of God. Bring your jars continually. As Jesus fills us with Himself, and the grace we need in that moment, we will not be in short supply. We will overflow!

Jesus has the final say. Nothing is over until He has completed

His will. Allow Jesus to invade your heart, and your marriage so much so that He fills you with all the fruit of the Spirit, in great abundance. Cast all your cares upon Him. Stop picking up fleeting thoughts and rooted emotions that are not meant for your good or your husband's good. Let go and let God!

To have unbelief about something in your life, comes from a fear of helplessness that you cannot do anything about it. As you surrender to God, 'believing for it' is actually the possible. Adopt a God-courage, God-faith, and God-worthiness for all that He is about to do in your heart. He is far greater than your belief and unbelief. Our belief, in and of ourselves, is faulty. We overthink, rationalize, justify, and placate. Read Ephesians 3:20.

Today, position your heart to abide on the vine, as God gives you His strength for what you are fasting and praying: overflowing unity, peace, harmony, connection, and healing.

Everyday in this prayer journal, you will discover more and more of your unraveling and unbecoming, met by even more of God's powerful, supernatural mending. Grant yourself patience and grace. This next caliber of spiritual maturity takes time. The more you allow God access to dig up ruts and cycles of unresolved pain within your heart, and the more you stop holding on to offenses, the messier it gets. Going deeper with God will unravel what no longer belongs. You will not feel comfortable with yourself until God sweeps the old away. It is sticky and cumbersome at first; and that's okay. Don't be afraid for what is yet to come. Believe for all that God is about to do in your heart, in your home, and in your marriage. Jesus will be with you always. I am praying for you, sis.

LISTEN & WATCH

1 Corinthians 13:7
Love bears all things, believes all things, hopes all things, endures all things.

Psalm 46:10
I am here, being still, knowing that you are God. As for me, my heart will be still.

Psalm 37:1-11
I wait patiently for you, not fretting over evildoers, not envious of wrongdoers, for they will soon fade like the grass, and I will be here, trusting in my Lord, delighting in Him. I refrain from anger...I will adopt meekness and walk in abundant peace.

Ephesians 6:10
Be strong in the Lord and in the strength of His might, not by my might or control.

PRAY: *BELIEVE FOR IT*

God, today I come before You with arms and heart open wide

for what Your will is, and for all of You to abide in all of me.

May Your presence transform me so that I know

Your heart and rise up in really believing for it!

I give to You what I am believing for in my marriage.

It's all Yours!

Praise You for being bigger than this mountain.

I don't care anymore how this mountain will be moved,

or that I don't know the way through, or that the tide has not

changed before, but I know that

I am on my knees before You,

believing for You to break these chains, & bust down locked doors.

Invade it all. You are the Way and You have the final say.

What has been immovable in my marriage,

in my husband, in me, I believe for the impossible to

become the possible today, God.

I declare my husband's victory because You said it is done.

All of the past is gone. I wage war on his behalf,

to trust You with him, that it's done, so that I can be his

embassador of hope, to usher in his miracle. God, I believe for it!

I stand in agreement with my God as I refuse anything

less than His will.

PRAYER *Woman*

JOURNAL PROMPT

Write out your prayer for believing for his miracle!

Write your prayer on accepting God's belief for your marriage.

DAY 4:
IDOLATRY & ADDICTION

Sister, I wanted to remind you that you are in a safe place. If you feel scared that your heart is hurting too much to let go of what you are doing to pacify the pain, I get it. It requires surrender to get free from your chains. I encourage you to be bold in your leap as you open your closed fists to God so that you can see beautiful again. You are not alone. Cutting out what does not belong is part of building a new path, where you will no longer feel the same about yourself. This is a process of eliminating things that are not honoring your true identity in Christ or the powerful purpose of your marriage. Digging deep always hurts our pride. If I could empower you with one lesson that set me free from my pain, it's this: you feel uncomfortable with your old you and that is fantastic, not worrisome. You feel pain because everything within you is being stripped down to your original design, and that is a growth pain. Sometimes shedding the old takes some good with it as it goes, because the two have been so deeply intertwined for so long. I want to encourage you that it is more than okay to release what you believe are the good parts of you during this journey. At first, I was very afraid to lose me, but as I leaned forward, it was fear holding me back from everything I wanted to become as a Godly woman.

There is no fear in the Love of God because when you lose yourself, you find more than enough in Him again. He is the Creator who holds all of who you are. I want this kind of love, how about you? If you feel stuck with circumstances and your feelings have such a tight grip around you that you are at an utter loss for how to take even a tiny step forward, I see you friend. This 41-day fast for unity in your marriage will bring to the surface both idols and addictions. Be on the alert as they present themselves with temptation and disguise their identity in rooted core beliefs. Ask Jesus to reveal to you the weeds that are rooted in your garden. We all have forms of idolatry: where things other than Jesus are getting our attention, time, resources, and energy. If we feel stuck in pain and cannot find victory, we have idolized the pain. It's time to confess and renounce what does not belong to your God-given purpose and identity. It's time to uproot and cleanse what no longer serves you for completing His will for the Kingdom, Prayer Woman. You are becoming a new woman. You have said *yes* to the new you. Are you ready to drop every single thing that He asks of you during this time? I know that you may be having some incredibly raw and real emotions as you pray for your heart and for your husband.

Maybe you are feeling unfairly treated, angry, or even emotionally paralyzed, traumatized, numb, or hopeless. I've been there. That weight will fall off under the blood of the Lamb and you will fly soon. Ponder the cost if you do not submit these obstacles to Jesu. You will still be stuck, spinning, lacking, hiding in fear, playing small, and unable to maximize your husband's potential if idols and addictions are in the way. Surrender, obey, and humble yourself. Stop blocking freedom. Idolatry is relying upon yourself to get you through instead of Abba. What are some ways that you idolize your beliefs, values, lifestyle, goals, finances, view of yourself, and view of marriage? Ask Jesus to show you the power of your fasting, which is abstaining from food and things that take time away from being with God. Fasting spiritually removes every obstacle and distraction that the devil plans to use to weaken you and keep you suppressed.
Let God shatter the strongholds.

LISTEN & WATCH

Psalm 34:8
Oh, taste and see that the Lord is good! Blessed is the man who takes refuge in Him!

Psalm 27:14
Wait for the Lord. Be strong and let your heart take courage; wait for the Lord!

Psalm 23:6
Surely goodness and mercy shall follow me all the days of my life, and I shall dwell in the house of the Lord forever.

Philippians 1:6
I am sure of this, that he who began a good work in you will bring it to completion at the day of Jesus Christ.

Philippians 2:13
For it is God who works in you, both to will and to work for His good pleasure.

1 Corinthians 10:24
Let no one seek his own good, but the good of his neighbor.

PRAY: *GOODNESS FOLLOWS HIM*

My husband is Your son, Abba. My covenant is from You.

You hold any good I can be and give.

May everything that flows from me, be from an

overflowing well of peace and gracefulness,

because I am a woman who *runs* to the living well.

My resources are never short or dry because I am a

PRAYER WOMAN who diligently runs after Your goodness.

It's here, in You, where I live and have my being.

Father, increase so that I may decrease.

Envelop me so that all of my needs, wants, and desires are

satisfied in You first, so that I can be about the

Kingdom business of pouring Your presence

over my husband, standing with him and for his good

rather than dragging him down with my selfish view.

Lord, forgive ungodly expectations.

I love how You are working in him to live in his

Godly role as my husband, as you are revealing to me the

Biblical wife role from Your Word. I am jubilant that

You are my Shepherd every step of the way.

I accept my prayer mantle.

I hide in You so that I am not hindering him

from Your glory, grace, blessing, and power.

JOURNAL PROMPT

What 3 areas in your life will you stop idolizing?

DAY 5:
REFINING FIRE

The fire...it's the tough spot, the imbalance of the yoke, the buried and soured offense, the bitter heart, the sickness, the loss, the lack, the trauma, the rejection or abandonment, the box people attempt to put you in to get you to react apart from Jesus. If you have known God for five weeks or five decades, you have also experienced a refining fire: a moment or season for which difficult situations form you. In both, He provides a way to develop character. Maybe that's not what you hoped when face with fire. A way out would be better perhaps. God's all consuming fire, however, is your way up, your way to give birth to fruit despite the scorching flames, wanting to consume what's inside. And what God is forming on the inside of you is beautiful.

The question is: will you allow the heat of life gone hard or gone wrong to produce an inner weariness or transform you? Some fire is from God, for your good, and other fire exists because we live in a broken world of sin, with an unleashed and roaming devil.

As a woman of prayer, it becomes crystal clear that every fiery dart meant to harm you can be disarmed or blocked. We disarm its threat for harm by adopting Jesus' perspective on its power: harmful only if you believe it rather than trust in God. We block it by having on our shield of faith and going to battle against it. In marriage, expect, for even a Godly marriage, to have these fiery darts of unkind words, selfishness, and pride. Knowing God means you have an identity in Christ to live out loud. It's then up to you to either step away from God's protection and become weary or put on the armor of God. Which one will you choose today?

In your walk with Jesus, it is in the *refining* for where God creates the rich portion for you - FILLED with love, to BE love, GIVE love, and DESIRE love. In the trials and tribulations, you will find the critical, turning away point of self and the open door for God's faithful and extravagant love. If He stood in the furnace of fire with Shadrach, Meshach, and Abednego, He will stand with you. Not only that, but you will come out of this not even smelling of smoke! Today, focus your time with Jesus for being open and thankful for the refining fire. To obtain a victory point in your marriage, for your husband to have victory in his battle, to find the way back to unity, the miracle: is to accept the crushing of what, how, when, and why you think it will occur. Remember, you are never alone and you are not the only one: Jesus was pierced for our transgressions and crushed for our iniquities. He went first.

In the exact moment, the hour of your devastation, in the breaking, crying & hyperventilating, Jesus is there. When you get on your knees to pray, Jesus can shift your pain, take it from you, and in exchange, charge you with an energy that propels you to run to bringing more light to your world. This has been my experience of knowing God: the place where He draws me out of my circumstance, and places my heart to stand on top of it. I do this by praying in a way that gives Jesus my anger, frustration, and sadness, all the feelings of my circumstance: *"Jesus, take everything that has been shot at me so that I don't hold it. Hide me in the shadow of Your wings."* And He does so, faithfully. By praying this, you just positioned yourself for immediate transformation and acceleration into hearing God's voice and the doing of His will for the Kingdom of Heaven.

LISTEN & WATCH

2 Corinthians 4:8
We are afflicted in every way, but not crushed; perplexed, but not driven to despair.

Isaiah 53:5
He was pierced for our transgressions; he was crushed for our iniquities; upon him was the chastisement that brought us peace, and with his wounds we are healed.

Psalm 119:140
Your promise is well tried, and your servant loves it.

Psalm 18:20
His way is perfect; the word of the Lord proves true; he is a shield for all those who take refuge in him.

Malachi 3:2
Who can endure the day of his coming, and who can stand when he appears? For he is like a refiner's fire and like fullers' soap.

PRAY: *REFINING FIRE*

Lord, I praise You for your mercies & peace. I love that You are my daily portion. I acknowledge and receive it today. Thank you for allowing hardship into my life, because when I stay in Your presence, all I see is mercy. All I see now is that You gave me this opportunity to need You. I trust that You have already been moving out ahead of me. As I remain in love with You, I know that whatever I face becomes like ash beneath my feet.

This refining fire hurts, but I know that it is my flesh burning away, not my spirit. My soul may feel injured and even broken, but I know who holds it, and I know whom is my Restorer.

Thank you, Abba, that you change my perspective in a moment, and are so faithful to take my pain in exchange for immediate hope. Right in the center of my trouble, I see You moving in me to dig this ditch. Here is the altar of my heart, so that You can provide my promise, even here in the testing, with my hand to the plow, in the middle of the fire. I dig to bury the old me, to plow here where it's barren. Lord, I empty my reactions to my situation, bury my offense and wrongdoings, and I ask for You to use this valley, my empty spaces, to come fill me with Your glory.

I use my faith-filled words to plant seeds of life.

My deficit, my vacancy, my fire, is the place where deliverance and freedom grow; right here, in this garden is where my Jesus transforms me.

JOURNAL PROMPT

What is being emptied out and how will you use your mouth to stir up the Spirit?

DAY 6:
HUMILITY: THE COST OF UNITY

Humility can be one of most difficult shifts in your spiritual growth, but if you put on the 'God goggles', as I like to call them, you will see your calling to humility in your marriage as the best path, and even, the easier path. If you hold on to beliefs and actions that are self-serving, you will grow weary and unable to endure hardship and loss. It took me a long time to learn this lesson because controlling how I got what I needed and wanted seemed to be the answer. Then, Holy Spirit taught me how to pray one of the most powerful prayers.

Pray with me:
"Lord, when I hold my answers in front of my face, it's all I can see and I become my own god, dictating what I need and how and when, but it has left me empty and in pain again, so I lay down my answers in exchange for yours. Show me Your way because I know it's better. I trust You with all of me and I relinquish my false rights over my life, even while I cannot see Your way."

The path of humility is truly easier because, there, you are aligned with God's power to move *for* your good. You are not alone in this mission. As you put God first and your husband second, give from God's well of living water. Be open and understanding to his needs. You are *on mission* with JESUS!

In Christ, these things get cancelled: difficulty, fear, and pride; so that we no longer wrestle with our flesh at the cost of losing the opportunity to esteem and respect your husband. When you remain hidden under God's wings, watch how He carries it for you. Yes, it still hurts, but remember, that it is probably your pride that is hurting, not you. Let the sifting of dross take its course. (1 Thessalonians 4:7) Let pride fall away. As you do, your days of heart pain begin to fall rapidly away. Hurt comes when we are not walking in humility. It comes when we cling to the things in our life that were never meant to be there in the first place. Be on the lookout for them; they will surface more and more during these 41 days of prayer and fasting.

As a wife, your submission is humility. The shackles of pride break when you acknowledge that humility is truly the way God intended for you from the beginning. Yes, you will have days, or even a moment right now, where you ask yourself if the cost for unity is actually worth it if it's going to take everything you think you want and need away from you. We are human; we want what we want. But, since the day you gave your life to Jesus, He became your Master. Now you get to live it out loud in your position as a wife. A life laid down.

The cost for unity is humility. It will require what you don't want to see or cannot fathom. You will have seasons of feeling like there is no point in giving up so much: all the good things and all of the unworthy things. That's right, those 'unworthy' beliefs too, because they are not needed at your destination. In the presence of God, He provides everything you need to fully operate as the Godly wife for which you are meant to be. Ask God to hold all of you, so that you are available to advocate unity for your marriage. He will do it! He does it every single time I ask Him, so I know that He will for you. I am praying for you, Prayer Woman!

LISTEN & WATCH

Philippians 2:3
Do nothing from selfish ambition or conceit, but in humility count others more significant than yourselves.

1 Peter 5:6
Humble yourselves, therefore, under the mighty hand of God so that at the proper time he may exalt you.

Ephesians 4:1-3
Walk in a manner worthy of the calling to which you have been called, with all humility and gentleness, with patience, bearing with one another in love, eager to maintain the unity of the Spirit in the bond of peace.

Proverbs 22:4
The reward for humility and fear of the Lord is riches and honor and life.

Colossians 3:14
Put on love, which binds everything together in perfect harmony.

PRAY: *THE COST IS MY HUMILITY*

Lord, I praise You for gifting to me my husband and the
calling on my life to be his support.
Here I am surrendering to you in ways I do not know exactly how
to do, but I know that You do. You know what it takes for me to
get past myself so that I can live a lifestyle of humility in
my marriage. I do not want even 99% humility, where I can still
reserve a little of me; I want the whole enchilada: 100%!!
You know what I will be going through to truly live from this
place, so I trust you. Take it all. I love you, God, more than
I love myself. I love your plan for my marriage more than
I love my own, so I ask for You to show me all of the areas that I
need to be humble enough so that You are glorified and my
husband is loved. What I don't have is no longer my focus.
You Agape Love has changed me.
Love has taken the ME out of me so that I can truly be a
Living Aura® & usher more of JESUS into my marriage.
I pray a powerful covering of peace over my husband right now
as You take what he clings to and turn it into open hands of his
surrender. We come to You open-handed, not holding plans,
unmet expectations, comparisons, or failures.
We open up our hearts and give You everything.
Lead my husband in humility and reward him favorably.
Everything he puts his hands upon will flourish.

JOURNAL PROMPT

List two ways you will show your husband humility today.

DAY 7:
I AM THE WARRIOR QUEEN

The wife is the prayer warrior queen of her household. She holds herself with dignity and takes her responsibility to defend truth very seriously. She girds her loins with strength and makes her arms strong. This means that the wife, as the Proverbs 31 woman, is intentional about being prepared for what she needs to handle and achieve. She doesn't walk into her day without priming herself for success. She is focused and not dismayed. Her spirit does not dwindle. It is strong and ready at all times. (Proverbs 31:18b)

Beautiful wife, you carry the authority to move mountains and make the impossible a possibility because of your connection to God. You maximize your husband's potential and usher agape love into your home. The warrior queen is strong and ready in her spirit: in the day, and in the night, in her gladness and in her despair, in moments of good and moments that can carry her away from peace. She stands fiercely.

> *"I am a woman of Faith! I believe for restoration, redemption, deliverance, repentance, humility, unity, and purity."*

The wife's mission carries the authority to crush the devil's head, carry the laurel crown of victory, & establish peace in your home. She wages war on the devil's head with wisdom. I wrote this down on my Day 7 of my fast for unity.

I encourage you to write down your own note in your journal, sticky note, mirror, or in the writing space on today's journal page: My job is to BE THE HOME:

a source of peace,
joyful no matter what, a believer in my husband,
carrier of my own energy, present and available;
face turned to Jesus

Woman of prayer, you'll be found on your knees, counting trials but joy, connected to the Father, and showing up in deeper and stronger growth today than the day before. Declare it now and keep going, every single day until you have completed these 41 days.

You can rise victoriously as the Warrior Queen for your soul, your home, and your husband because Jesus first won the war for you! Partner in that power. Nothing can separate you from the love of God. Knowing this, God did not set you up for failure. He is your promise of success. He knows the exact battle you will face, and the battles that were never meant for you.

Sometimes, we can shift into intercession mode for a battle that was never meant for us to war, so using discernment and wisdom is the key to having the peace of His promise.

Knowing your battles means having the grace and peace and power from Jesus (not of yourself) to overcome. Choosing your battles means knowing when to hold your tongue and when to speak up but with grace and wisdom. In prayer, you will determine the difference.

LISTEN & WATCH

Colossians 2:6,7,9,10
As you received Christ Jesus the Lord, so walk in Him, rooted and built up in Him and established in the faith, just as you were taught, abounding in thanksgiving...For in Him the whole fullness of deity dwells bodily, and you have been filled in Him, who is the head of all rule and authority.

John 17: 2,3
Since You have given Him authority over all flesh, to give eternal life to all whom You have given Him. And this is eternal life, that they who know you, the only true God...

Luke 10:19
I have given you authority to trample on snakes and scorpions, and to overcome the power of the enemy; nothing shall harm you.

Psalm 89:18
Our shield belongs to the Lord.

2 Chronicles 20:15
Do not be afraid nor dismayed at this great horde, for the battle is not yours but God's.

PRAY: *WARRIOR QUEEN*

Jesus, thank you that You are my reason for

believing in victory. You hold my battles because

You hold the whole war. As a prayer warrior queen,

You are my defender, my foundation, my hope, and my King.

Today, I don't fight any battles that You have

not already won for me.

I say YES to the promises on the other side of my

husband's victory. If he hasn't seen them yet,

I lean into faith on his behalf, and offer my yes and amen.

I do not grow weary or get caught off guard because

You make me awake to the power inside my role as a Godly wife.

I tap into Your power, Jesus, as my daily bread,

so that You can come and do ALL that You came to do.

I choose forgiveness for my past, my husband's past,

forgiveness of people and situations that didn't bear Godly fruit,

and I get into alignment with Your promises,

crowned with laurel leaves,

a Warrioress in the Kingdom of Heaven.

NOTHING can keep freedom from my marriage.

I stand up fiercely for my husband's heart, and act

as the ambassador of God's agape love

so that his potential is maximized and favored.

Together, we battle!

JOURNAL PROMPT

Write out your battle cry prayer for your husband.

DAY 8:
MARRIED ON MISSION

Are you hungry to make a significant impact on the Kingdom of Heaven? Have you been wondering what it looks like for your purpose as a Godly wife to be eternity driven? Once you accept and receive that you are fully known by the God of the Universe, you begin to walk more confidently and purposefully on MISSION. *Married On Mission* is now your motto.

Today, put on the eternity mindset for your marriage. You are now being driven in a vehicle to a new destination. What this means is your God-given mission now supercedes any of your personal dreams, agendas, earthly accomplishments or assets. God's eternal mission is your supernatural destiny.

As we travel through our lifetime, we pass through many seasons of change and growth, with both victories and losses. We discover seasonal purpose inside these life chapters, then they come to a close. But when you're married, this mission mindset begins to permeate at a foundational, lifetime level that drives your decisions, motives, energy, and perspectives.

When we face a challenge, we go through some fire. We might even become afraid or changed by it, but we always come out of it one way or another. In my worst moments of tragedy, change, trial, and trauma, I've noticed a trend to set in as I became this kind of PRAYER WOMAN....My mindset shifted from devastation to thankfulness. Now, because of the transformational belief that you are Married On Mission, it will give you a powerful stance for taking on any and every challenge as a thankful praise. God mercifully allows you to experience it *so that* you can need Him, run to Him, and be found in Him.

It is no longer a scary place to face trials because you get to run to Jesus, the living well of everlasting fruit...keyword: *get* to! Jesus' merciful outpouring of love is seen when facing blinding pain because it is in these sweet moments, in the middle of the storm, where we run to our knees and face and cry out to Abba, that He meets us, and in a moment, shifts all lack of our understanding and offers His peace. He also gives a supernatural surge of energy to go be about His business.

When you become mission-minded, you are able to extend beyond your own needs, even the immediate needs of your household. Married on Mission is grounded in God's work, so while you go out into the earth to be the salt, the light, and bring God's hope to a hurting world, God is working in your heart for your marriage. Even in the middle of chaos there is a loving and available God who readily shifts every amount of pain and tears you've shed, and turns it into a powerful expression of joy and love in this mission. This is literally the BEST NEWS EVER!

God truly gave you not just good news, but the best news ever! There is always a way. You are never cornered or lost and up the creek with no paddle. He is there, right in the middle and ahead of you, perfectly crafting your position to walk mightily and confidently in your married mission. This M.O.M. framework solves doubt, worry, fear, inadequacy, unworthiness, and more. You are called for such a time as this, Queen!

LISTEN & WATCH

Lamentations 3:22
The steadfast love of the Lord never ceases; his mercies never come to an end.
Psalm 21:7
For the king trusts in the Lord, and through the steadfast love of the Most High he shall not be moved.
Proverbs 31:11
The heart of her husband trusts in her, and he will have no lack of gain.
Proverbs 31:31
Give her the fruit of her hands, and let her own works praise her in the gates.
Proverbs 12:4a
An excellent wife is the crown of her husband.
1 Peter 3:1
They see your respectful and pure conduct.

PRAY: *ON MISSION*

Jesus, You are a Great God, who knew before my time what

my mission would be as the wife to my husband.

You saw the place I would stand. You began to work in

me years before I was positioned. You went ahead of me

to carve and craft such a perfect spot just for me alone,

here, as my husband's forever divine mate.

You call me Great Wife and Beloved Daughter.

I know that I was sent on mission for such a time as this.

There is no other place for me. I am on assignment to be Love,

because God is in me and He is Love.

I cannot be separated from the love of the Lord.

Jesus, I praise You for being Love, so that when I look at

myself in the mirror, I fill up with Joy because I see Your handiwork.

Lord, be my husband's JOY!

Bubble up within his soul today

a deep well of everlasting love; a love so radiant and pure,

a generous love. Lead him as he leads me through a

life that is poured out on our Jesus mission.

Strengthen his leadership of

faithfulness, forgiveness, surrender, submission,

forbearance, chastity, and holiness before the Lord.

Lead him with compassion and pure devotion.

Show him the details of Your mission. Speak Your will.

JOURNAL PROMPT

Write your declaration for being on a married mission.

DAY 9:
TRUSTING GOD

The key to unleashing God's strength in your weariness and weakness is: TRUSTING God in the middle of it all. Let go of control, because it is a huge hindrance to unity in marriage. When I was younger, I used control to benefit me and thought it was actually good because I had mixed it so well with my identity. I had deep-seeded heart belief that I needed to control everything. Somehow, I had told myself narratives that I needed to secure x,y, and z because 'that's who I am', 'it's good for me', 'nobody can take that from me', and for some things I even went so far as to tell myself 'it's how God made me, with this gift.' Can you relate? In your marriage, what areas have brought you abruptly to a wall of 'no'? We hit 'NOs' when we bank on ourselves; where we force unhealthy situations because we do not allow anyone in other than the big "ME"! There it is again: *me*. As a Godly wife, you can not afford to give lip service for trusting in God, while secretly working on a situation in your favor. We either trust God all the way, or we don't. Cling to purity in your trust walk.

Trusting God is your first step to trusting your husband. If you are not trusting your husband as the head of the household, as is his Godly domain, then the root cause is probably that you do not know how to trust God. Work it out in prayer. Today, our focus is not about you learning to trust your husband more; that will happen on its own when you first TRUST GOD! As a Prayer Woman, stand upon the Word of God for His answers, lean in to soaking in Jesus' presence, and run to His well for your filling. We must continually run to the living well so that we have what it takes to answer our husbands in trust and with spiritual fruit. If we cannot answer with grace in our speech, respond with a joyful spirit, and trust God wholeheartedly, *run* to prayer where only Jesus can fill those dry cisterns. In Jesus, you will find comfort. The power that allows you to soar in your circumstance is supernatural, but you cannot live out your Godly role as a wife if you aren't placing your trust in God.

Trusting God is waiting upon Him. Trust says *yes*! Trust enables, it frees, it listens, it allows my husband to be and live out his position and ALL that God wants him to be as the head of the wife. Trusting God is bringing what you need to God and letting go of it, leaving it on that floor where you knelt to pray. Trusting God is resolving that God is Bigger than all of it. Trusting God does not take the hardship away: it refines you. When you trust in Jesus first, He shows you how to trust in your husband, and from this place in Jesus, you become trustful and trustworthy.

Instead of trying in your own might and mental capacity to trust your husband, start with trusting God! Father will work in you to absolve the belief patterns and reasons for mistrust. Cry on Jesus. Don't go to your husband in an attempt to confront him on misplaced trust. Give it all to Jesus. Become the wife who fully relies upon Jesus, then watch how the Holy Spirit radically it shifts your husband into a trust-filled marriage. Lead by example. Honor your heart and identity in Christ. You can live yielded, Prayer Woman, because God will take care of you. Trusting is emptying yourself completely in the loving arms of the Good Shepherd. It can be messy and painful, but then He sets you free from the flesh, and trusting becomes easy as His yoke is easy and His burden is light.

LISTEN & WATCH

Lamentations 3:37
Who has spoken and it came to pass, unless the Lord has commanded it?
Proverbs 3:5 Trust in the Lord with all your heart, and do not lean on your own understanding.
Romans 8:28
We know that for those who love God all things work together for good, for those who are called according to His purpose.
Luke 15:10
The one who is faithful in very little is also faithful in much, and one who is dishonest in very little is also dishonest in much.
Jeremiah 17:7,8
Blessed is the man who trusts in the Lord, whose trust is in the Lord. He is like a tree planted by water, that sends out its roots by stream, and does not fear...
Psalm 56:3 When I am afraid, I put my trust in you.
Isaiah 26:3,4
You keep him in perfect peace whose mind is stayed on you, because he trusts in you. Trust in the Lord forever, for the Lord God is an everlasting rock.

PRAY: *I TRUST JESUS*

I trust You, Father. I trust You when I wake and when I sleep. I trust you when I don't see answers and when I do. I trust You with my marriage and for how Sovereign You are. God, you know the number of the stars in the universe, you feed every sparrow, and you know the details in my marriage. So, trusting You is easy, and I rejoice that my understanding is finite and Yours is not. Create in me a clean heart, capable of being a trustworthy wife for my husband. Show me what he needs, God.

Seal this trust as far as the east is from the west; no digging up the old. Show me how to be his safe place of rest. Keep him close to Your heart so that He can be close to me. Deliver him from every cycle of mistrust, and lead him into a bountiful harvest of safety. Wrap Your loving arms around him so that everything in him that is not for his good becomes loosened and falls at his feet. Turn to ash what no longer serves where You are taking him in his journey of trusting You and trusting me. Show him your Sovereignty and Safety; that trusting You leads to the fullness of life. You are the Way, the Truth, and the Life. You are King of his heart, and I praise you for being my husband's everything. May my submission to You enable him to flow in all that You are making in him for Godliness.

Protect him as he trusts in You.

JOURNAL PROMPT

What are you trusting in God for today?

DAY 10:
SOW WHAT YOU WANT TO HARVEST

Take time to ponder what you need to sow into this prayer journey? Ask Jesus what He wants you to sow so that His will can be done, then, walk in it faithfully.

There are sowers, and there are reapers. If you want to be treated with kind words, be the woman who is first to speak those kind words. If you need gentleness, do not return anger for anger. Instead, sow the fruit, and do not stop sowing no matter how long the harvest takes. If you get tired, if you are at the end of your rope, if you are at full bandwidth, or find yourself justifying how much you have poured out in relation to what you are not getting back: STOP! Stop the measuring. Stop the retaliation, fairness, & counter-attacks. This is not your position as a Godly wife.

In Luke 6:31, it says that "As you wish what others would do to you, do so to them." Also, in verse 29, "to the one who strikes you on the cheek, offer the other also, and from one who takes away your cloak do not withhold your tunic also."

Remember, that as God's own daughter, you belong to the Kingdom of Heaven and the fullness of it. So, no matter what you believe is being taken from you, or happening against you, your actions are to only come from God's living well, because it is there where you abide, and there, alone, where you get the seeds to sow into your covenant marriage. Go on sowing spiritual goodness and setting the Living Aura® from the living well of Jesus. Sow Jesus, not you.

If Father God provides for the sparrows and lilies of the valley, He will do so for you, so there is no more fear in sowing what God tells you to sow, no matter how big the ask feels. All of your needs will be met by the King of Heaven, not by you reserving and holding back. If you are in lack, empty, and needing to be fed by more patience, intimacy, comfort, or unity with your covenant partner, then run to Abba and be filled. Truly, everything You need is in Jesus. He can take all of your needs and provide supernatural fulfillment to you while He goes on your behalf to your husband and, as only God can do, grant him a measure of awakening, ability, desire, and courage to come to you. And where will your husband find you? On your knees, praying: full of Jesus, not nagging, begging, or lacking.

If you need intimacy...
If you desire to be admired and shown affection...
If you crave to be known...
If your heart needs to be heard and held...
If you desire love and peace...
If it's been awhile since he was thoughtful or kind...
Run to the WELL of JESUS! Living as a well watered woman is drinking from His everlasting resources and trusting that He is enough. Just because you are married, it does not mean that your needs stop being met by Jesus FIRST!

If there is any shortcoming, lack, rejection, miscommunication, abandonment, distance, or cold war that is witholding the Godly blessings of marriage, then stare at Jesus' face until HE moves in your husband for you. Rest in Jesus and God will complete His will. The Prayer Woman's position is to take her needs to Abba first and let go in His presence!

LISTEN & WATCH

Galatians 6:8
For the one who sows to his own flesh will from the flesh reap corruption, but the one who sows to the Spirit will from the Spirit reap eternal life.

Mark 4:3,8
A sower went out to sow. Seeds fell into good soil and produced grain, growing up and increasing and yielding thirty-fold and sixtyfold and a hundredfold.

Psalm 126:5
Those who sow in tears shall reap with shouts of joy!

Galatians 5:16
Walk by the Spirit, and you will not gratify the desires of the flesh. For the desires of the flesh are against the Spirit, and the desires of the Spirit are against the flesh...

Mark 12: 31
The second is this: 'You shall love your neighbor as yourself.' There is no other commandment greater than these.

Galatians 5:22,23
The fruit of the Spirit is love, joy, peace, patience, kindness, goodness, faithfulness, gentleness, self-control; against such things there is no law. Those who belong to Christ Jesus have crucified the flesh with its passions and desires.

PRAY: *SOWING REAL FRUIT*

I sow love, joy, peace, patience, kindness, goodness, faithfulness, gentleness, and self-control into my husband. Grant me more of these real and lasting fruits from my time spent with You. I choose to sow in the Spirit rather than in my flesh, to love my neighbor, who is my husband, as You love him. Guide my husband to walk in the Holy Spirit, resist the devil, and flow in the blessing of being pure in heart. I commit to sow into my husband from God alone as I submit my needs to Jesus.

May my husband walk joyfully with praise as his weapon. Keep him rooted in humility, kindness, and gentleness and break off every trigger and pain point that is attempting to keep him tied down, numb, blind, and unable to pour out from a place of healing, from the place of fullness that You have for him. Give him the vision that You've cancelled every giant's power, and grant him the courage to adopt all Your fruits as he keeps You first. I pray a hedge of protection around my husband during his journey of transformation from flesh to Spirit.

Draw him to closer to You. Help me be consistent in my obedience to operating from the fruit of the Spirit, that it may give him the safe place He needs to change and mature. May the lamp of his soul be sustained and not grow dim. Show him the bountiful harvest found only in sowing in the Spirit.

JOURNAL PROMPT

What can you sow into your husband today?

DAY 11:
EXPECT TO BE TIRED

Are you tired yet?

I know the feeling, lady! When I first went through this fast and prayer walk, my spirit was activated into high gear, and the attacks that came after me, were greater than before I had started.

Say this with me:

> *"I am committed to*
> *this process, and everything*
> *God wants to do,*
> *He can, because I am not quitting."*

Expect to be tired physically and emotionally when you are purposeful in your mission for more unity in your marriage, because you are emptying out everything that does not belong. You are inviting God to partner with you in forging new paths, clearing, sifting, and conquering.

Give yourself extra time today, if you can, to take a nap, even if it's only a twenty minute shut-eye. If you need to set up a board game or book time for your young children or reschedule a work appointment, do so. Your energy is pivotal to how well you do through this prayer journey. Turn on soaking, worship music and let the peace of God consume you. Become a woman who prepares spaces in her day for all the responsibilities to flow from a place, first found by seeking God's face. It is there, in your time with Jesus, where you find the kind of rest that sustains like no other. Lay down at the Lord's feet everything that keeps you busy, tired, and emotionally distrought; and rest in the center of the storm, here in Jesus' heart. In the middle of it all, He satisfies, renews, and fills us like a refreshing drink. Come near the river of life.

A Proverbs 31 woman is prepared, her household is maintained, yes, but in order for her to do this, you first put on your own oxygen mask. It is imperative to rest and take it easier today.

A well-rested woman can conquer more than she knows, just in her rest-filled being, than in her do-it-all mentality. Being rested will center your peace, and rejuvenate you on a molecular and neurovascular level.

Your prayer woman journey is more about BEING than you know. Be today! Be all of You!

HE WHO FINDS A
GOOD

Wife

FINDS A GOOD
THING AND
OBTAINS FAVOR
FROM THE LORD.

PROVERBS 18:22

LISTEN & WATCH

Isaiah 26:3
You keep him in perfect peace whose mind is stayed on you, because he trusts in you.

2 Corinthians 12:9
He said to me, "My grace is sufficient for you, for my power is made perfect in weakness." Therefore, I will boast all the more gladly of my weaknesses, so that the power of Christ may rest upon me.

Matthew 11:28,30
Come to me, all who labor and are heavy laden, and I will give you rest. For my yoke is easy, and my burden is light.

Hebrews 4:10
Whoever has entered God's rest has also rested from his works as God did from his.

PRAY: *RESTING*

Abba, you rested on Day 7 of creation.

Thank you for giving me the example to take care of me

and protect my energy as well as my inner peace.

I press in to all that You want to show me on *rest*.

You know how tired I am. The attacks have not let up.

It's weighing down on my spirit, where I'm running to

You constantly for resources, but oh wow, it's a lot, and my

body feels the exercise of my spirit. Make me stronger.

Grant me rest in body, mind, soul, and spirit today!

Watch over me, guard and protect me as I rest.

I know how vital it is to protect my health

because the devil is waiting to creep into any tiny crevice of

weakness that comes in being tired.

I, actively, pursue Your perfect protection today.

Come rejuvenate me spiritually, emotionally;

touch my organs, systems, bones, and brain with perfect peace.

Guard my husband in your shalom so that he is also blessed.

Revive my husband on a molecular level, to be radiant in You.

Give him Your strength. Protect him in health.

As he sleeps tonight, may his spirit and soul rest as You lavish

upon him supernatural rejuvination. Make his load be made light

and His paths narrow and straight.

JOURNAL PROMPT

How will you rest today? I give you permission.

DAY 12:
EXPECT ADVERSITY

Adversity comes in all forms and sizes and seasons. Sometimes it comes in the most unexpected condition or from a person you least expect; like a family member or best friend. Adversity has no barometer of force upon its subject. It doesn't hold out from the weak or the person who is in the midst of a life celebration. It comes without warning, to all.

Adversity, by definition, is an unfortunate event, marked by misfortune, calamity, or distress. So, it can come into our life from things that happen to us, but I want to point out that it is our responsibility, as Godly wives, to do with it then as we must. Our answer to calamity is where we can rise or fall. What will be your response? Adversity can come from a choice to take offense or realize that God is bigger. Adversity can also come to us where it seems like we have no choice but to face it. We do have a choice for the position of our spirit inside the known adversity. Will you do it with Jesus?

Yes, being married, you will be tried and tested beyond what you think you can bear. I used to get disturbed by the phrase, "He will never give me anything that is too difficult" because I have been broken so many times before. But when I went into God's Word, I found that it says, He will "not allow you to be tempted beyond what you are able". That's different because God always provides a way of escape, whether that is in gaining His perspective, finding shelter in His presence, or having a miracle knock at your front door today.

Adopt His presence and your hope will expand beyond the adversity. You will be pushed past your limits, and in this space you will find God. Yes, it is a space where YOU don't have control, but as you cling to Jesus, He offers a peace that surpasses your current understanding.

God has the big picture so that you can live beyond your own understanding and control. As you answer from God' Spirit, you will find His abounding peace. Even in the midst of adversities: the loss of a child, illness, rape, divorce, hate, pride, crime, abandonment, rejection, or the loss of income. Yes, adversity is in this world. What will your spirit's response become? Ask yourself, will I rise in peace or will I fall into chaos? While you cannot change the reality of walking through the storm, here are your new pair of goggles: from me to you. Try them on for a moment. Through this lens you'll see that there is a different space to stand in, which offers peace and endurance, a quiet knowing that while you have no control, God has it all and that is more than enough. So, are you needing help today? Put on His lens of good news. It's not a religious sentence to repeat until a light bulb goes off. This is a relationship with Jesus and it's alive. There is a space in God's heart for you that is so much bigger than you can comprehend. His plan for you is beyond this adversity.

It only takes the size of a mustard seed of faith in God to move mountains. If all you can do is just tell Him "I trust you, God, and allow You to be the One to show me the *how* of trusting in You", He is faithful to do so.

LISTEN & WATCH

Isaiah 40:29,31
To those who have no might He increases strength. Those who wait upon the Lord shall renew their strength, they shall mount up with wings like eagles, they shall run and not be weary, they shall walk and not faint.

Psalm 27:32,14
I believe that I shall look upon the goodness of the Lord in the land of the living. Wait for the Lord; be strong, and let your heart take courage.

Lamentations 3:25
The Lord is good to those who wait for Him: to the soul who seeks Him.

Proverbs 3:5,6
Trust in the Lord with all your heart, and lean not on your own understanding. In all your ways, acknowledge Him, and He shall direct your paths.

1 Corinthians 10:12,13
Therefore, let him who thinks he stands take heed lest he fall. No temptation has overtaken you except such as is common to man; but God is faithful, who will not allow you to be tempted beyond what you are able, but with the temptation will also make the way of escape, that you may be able to bear it.

PRAY: *I AM STILL*

As I am still, in your presence, I know where I am, whose I am,
and that everything I need You already have.
So, I agree with Your almighty provision for my own needs,
I pause, I am still. I give You control over my life.
I give You the outcome, the timing, and the way for Your glory.
Lord, here I am, laying down all of the me that wants me.
I come to You as a vessel of intercession for my husband.
Rush in to him, wherever he is right now, and offer the riches
of Peace from Your abundant warehouse.
God, you never run dry. You create something out of nothing.
You are the Peace in the center of adversity, so I align my prayers
to faith, asking for Jesus to unleash a downpour of what only You
can provide. Your outcome far surpasses what I have faith for or
can imagine. Your outcome for my husband in this circumstance
is much bigger than it all, so I say "YES" to it, no matter what it
looks like. You are God. Go God!
Unleash his full potential, even now, in the middle of it.
Thank you for endurance in this race.
Spirit of God, crush all fear, pride, & selfishness that may cause a
hindrance for my husband's victory and blessing.
Come do what You came to do; only You can.

JOURNAL PROMPT

How will you be STILL today?

DAY 13:
GOD HOLDS THE OUTCOME

As a disciple of the Gospel of Christ, your life belongs to God. He holds the beginning, the middle, and the end. He holds the unknown and the known. When you do not know the outcome, God does. This offers every assurance that the day is known, and everything needed for victory and glory is available to you. When you woke up today, and got out of bed, your feet hit the floor. As you walk, His victory and peace is made available to you.

Rise up and step into a purposeful and intentional position that God has prepared for you. You are equipped by God in all things when you abide on the vine with Him. So, no matter what happens in your day, from the moment your feet hit the floor, that Prayer Woman is ready! She knows how to respond in the Spirit of God... when she receives that unexpected phone call, when slander is thrown, when a loved one slips back into sin, when kindness is not repaid. He is with you in the in-betweens, while you're waiting for the miracle.

I, too, have experienced heartache from placing my desired outcome above God's will. Self-induced heartache is misalignment & disobedience. The moment you are resolved for belonging to Jesus 100%, is the moment He can take that self-sabotaging pain from your life and be the Lord of it. There was a time, in my marriage, when I was misguided and narrow-minded in my emotions about my circumstance. I had to surrender my flesh and acknowledge Jesus' will as sovereign. The place where you step away from control and into a beautiful surrender is truly marvelous!

What this means is that when you feel the pain from controlling the outcome, which is an idol (Day 4), and it's swarming in and around your heart, the only reason it can mature is by way of you feeding it. We do so by over-thinking, making excuses, validating emotions, and by adopting it as the position for bringing about change on our own. This will bring failure and leave you feeling miserable because it was never God's design for you to control what happens next.

Today, say YES to God holding your outcome! If you hold on to what you want for your heart, for your marriage, or for your husband, what is the cost? It may sound good. Your hope may even be good. But if it is not submitted to God, even a good desire can be captivated by ego. Without complete surrender and submission, you are the cause of blocking unity and blessing in your marriage. Every good and every perfect gift comes down from the Father of Lights.

DECLARE: *this marriage belongs to God and He will have His way. Move me or move the mountain, but it will be done.* Your submission is the position your spirit takes for God to hold the outcome. It comes with great favor! The favor of the Lord is a presence that follows you, finds you, wars on your behalf, and brings a bountiful harvest to you and your marriage.

The PRAYER WOMAN prays with a surrendered heart, for God's will instead of yours. Take your heart to the safety and shelter of His wings. He will always listen. He knows you better than you know yourself. He gives you more than you deserve, and helps guide you and hold you every step of the way. After all, this life on earth is for Him. It's not about what we can get out of it.

LISTEN & WATCH

Psalm 52:8
I trust in the steadfast love of God forever and ever.
2 Thessalonians 3:5
May the Lord direct your hearts to the love of God...
1 John 5:3
For this is the love of God, that we keep his commandments. And His commandments are not burdensome.
Ephesians 3:19
...to know the love of Christ that surpasses knowledge, that you may be filled with all the fullness of God.
Jude 1:21
Keep yourselves in the love of God, waiting for mercy of our Lord Jesus Christ that leads to eternal life.
Matthew 6:10
Your kingdom come, your will be done, on earth as it is in heaven.

PRAY: *GOD IS IN CONTROL*

I repent of fear gripping my heart, and fervently pursue finding

Jesus instead. Here, is where I now surrender every worry.

The overthinking of my situation and trying to work it out on my

own, is the old me. Now, I choose to surrender and be still with

Jesus. It's only here, where every fear falls into perfect peace, and

where Jesus shows me that He has won the war. Every wall I face,

He dissolves. Every giant falls. One by one, my plans and worries,

needs and wants, they belong to Jesus now. When my heart feels

restriction, I yield to Father. He holds it all for me, reminds me of

who I am. He goes to battle on behalf of my husband. Father holds

his anxious thoughts, until all that's left is peace. You keep his

heart and mind still so that he can breathe You in, Jesus.

Make Your will known to my husband so that You are the reason

he leads with excellence. May peace course through his being.

May protection be upon him all day. I thank you, God,

that even if nothing changes about the outcome, that my

husband still praises You and faithfully walks as Your servant.

May his surrender grow everyday, protected and nurtured in You.

Keep speaking to him as he comes and as he goes.

In the quiet and in the noise, be there for him.

Show up in big ways, God. Make Your way known to him.

Thank you for his good covering over me.

JOURNAL PROMPT

What area of your life will you yield to God?

DAY 14:
AT THE CROSS

Jesus gave us the perfect example of a life laid down when He gave Himself as the ultimate sacrifice on the cross. On Day 14, in the very first Prayer Woman fast I did, Jesus revealed to me the transformational power of the cross as it pertains to how He created marriage. Jesus paid the price and *still* gave us the option to receive His free gift of salvation. He generously granted us the gift of grace, regardless of whether we would accept it or not, demonstrating that God's kindness was not dependent upon our willingness to receive it. He gave Himself and opened the door for our way back to Heaven. Even when we were the ones who sinned in the first place, He took it upon Himself to make it right. Why? Because He is Love! This is His great rescue story for us.

With this in mind, now we can view our marriage through the eyes of Love. If God showed His love to us while we were still sinners, died for us, gave His all, just for us to have a way back to eternity with Him, can you offer grace to your husband even if he doesn't always know how to receive it? Similarly, how will you receive the gift of your husband's life laid down for you as your covering, which is His God-given role?

A husband's role, according to Ephesians 5:25-27, is to "love his wife as Christ loved the church and gave himself up for her, that he might sanctify her, having cleansed her by the washing of water with the Word." The Scripture is clear for a husband's role in his marriage; to lay down his life for her, to love her as he loves his own body, just as Christ does the church.

The Godly husband continually draws upon the strength of the cross and its significance. And even if and when he does not, will you accept the power of the cross in your marriage? Will you allow Jesus' love on the cross to be your example for fully and unconditionally respecting your husband, no matter how rich or how poor his heart attitude is in his God mission? Yes, Prayer Woman! You can! You have the power of the cross.

Draw your strength from the Blood of the Lamb. What happened there is that ALL sin, yours and his, past and future, they all came under submission to what Jesus did - and He set us free! It is final so you can't keep holding that sin over your husband's head and reacting to a sin for which redemption has been served.

The freedom is in the cross. It's our behavior that must catch up to where our spirit dwells. As a Gody wife, you get to receive from God then give to your husband, yes, from that place of grace and redemption. You don't get to stop respecting and forgiving when you feel like it. For me, the hardest time to continue giving mercy and kindness and all those beautiful fruits of the Spirit, is when I am holding in front of me something I cannot release to God. For example, you might be seeing his attitude, his poor judgment, his this or that, but that all doesn't matter for how you respond to him. I know, it can feel tough at first. But, I promise, the more time you spend with Jesus, the easier giving and being becomes. Father teaches you how to abide in Him. You are connected.

Go ahead, and get to the end of yourself, beloved daughter. God already paved the way. I am cheering for you! This is your Living Aura®.

LISTEN & WATCH

Galatians 2:20
I have been crucified with Christ. It is no longer I who live, but Christ who lives in me. And the life I now live in the flesh I live by faith in the Son of God, who loved me and gave Himself for me.

Romans 5:8
God shows His love for us in that while we were still sinners, Christ died for us.

1 Peter 2:24
He Himself bore our sins in His body on the tree, that we might die to sin and live to righteousness. By His wounds you have been healed.

Matthew 10:38
Whoever does not take up his cross and follow me is not worthy of me.

Ephesians 5:25-27

Ephesians 2:8
For by grace you have been saved through faith. And this is not your doing; it is the gift of God.

PRAY: *THE CROSS*

Thank You, Jesus, for giving us the example of a way that

does not bar us from getting back to a place of redemption,

no matter how much we have sinned.

Thank you that no matter my error, my sin, or my husband's, that

there is nothing that can stop the love of God. There is nothing

hindering us from living inside a thriving love-filled marriage,

because You have already put to death the flesh.

I come before You, my spirit aligned with Your Truth,

and ask for a covering over my husband today:

that You would protect him as he draws upon the power of

the cross. May He know this power, be transformed even more,

and be enthralled in the great victory

You have won for him and for us!

Thank you for the cross. Thank you for overcoming sin so that we

can come freely to You, so that we can be washed by the blood of

the Lamb, and view each other as being so, no longer holding any

sin over each other's head. For You already came that we might

live in harmony, unity, peace, and abiding love.

Praise You, Abba, for this miraculous mystery!

Reveal the cross to my husband today, that he might

live fully alive in his role as an Ephesians 5 husband.

JOURNAL PROMPT

How is the cross breaking down walls for you?

DAY 15:
FAITH AND ACTION

In the book of James, he describes that faith without works is useless or dead. As Abraham offered up his son, Isaac, on the altar, he acted in *obedience* to God, but the Bible also says that Abraham had **faith** all along **with** his **works**, and that faith was completed by his works - and that God called Abraham: *friend*. How beautiful!

I use this Biblical example for our lesson today on FAITH AND ACTION because it is an excellent, unequivocal answer for how the wife's role in this can be both life and death. The virtuous wife intentionally walks in her purpose as God's workmanship; created in Christ Jesus for good works, which God prepared beforehand, that she should walk in them. (Ephesians 2:10)

The Prayer Woman does not stop at only knowing *about* faith, or using her faith only to pray, in addition, she applies herself to *doing* good all the days of her life. She puts her hand to the plow, to create time in her routine for putting and keeping Jesus first and her husband second. She is healthy and rested so that she is prepared, level-headed, disciplined, and orderly, knowing that in everything she does, is worship unto the Lord.

Even when I am washing the dishes, sweeping the stairs, folding laundry, planning another business launch, writing my husband a love & gratitude note - all of these minute and extravagant actions are done unto the Lord, with joy and thankfulness. I get to use all that I am and do it while fellowshipping with Abba. I get to serve because Jesus served first.

The wife has faith that no matter how little her works may seem, or how large the platform she produces, that ALL things work together for her good because she loves God. A Prayer Woman's love and devotion for God in this way is her devotion to ushering glory to God and blessing to her husband.

> *Wives,*
> *submit to your*
> *own husbands,*
> *as unto the Lord.*
> EPHESIANS 5:22

The husband is indirectly blessed through her faithful action being unto the Lord. The keyphrase I am highlighting here is that last line: "as unto the Lord". If your submission is first and foremost to the Lord, then you have nothing to fear for yourself.

If we do not have faith and action from a heart that willingly gives to the Lord, you may experience obstacles. The problem is that we will always fail to continually produce good works and good fruit if it comes from ourselves. Get out of your own way! Stop fixing the problems, and begin to worship. Worship with full faith in a God who is the Way and who creates new paths for us. Faith says no to the old patterns, excuses, and offense. It belongs to the Lord.

Today, put Jesus first in all that you do and believe for, and watch how God unleashes greater potential for moving mountains in your marriage and beyond.

LISTEN & WATCH

Hebrews 11:6
And without faith it is impossible to please Him, for whoever would draw near to God must believe that he exists and that he rewards those who diligently seek Him.

Matthew 21:21
"Truly, I say to you, if you have faith and do not doubt, you will not only do what has been done to the fig tree, but even if you say to this mountain, 'Be taken up and thrown into the sea,' it will happen.

James 2:17
Faith by itself, if it does not have works, it is dead.

James 1:3
For you know that the testing of your faith produces steadfastness

Romans 10:17
Faith comes from hearing, and hearing through the Word of God.

PRAY: *FAITH IN GOD & FOR MY HUSBAND*

Lord, search me and know me. Come purify my heart

that I may be acceptable in Your sight.

May the words of my mouth and the meditations

of my heart be acceptable in Your sight,

O Lord, my Rock and my Redeemer. (Psalm 19:14)

May all that I do be unto You, Lord.

Teach me how to listen and know Your still voice

so that in everything I do, I bless Your name, and

am a blessing to my husband.

May everything that my husband puts his hands upon bless

Your name: in his workplace, projects, relationships,

mind and soul. Delight in the sweet aroma from his devotion

to You. I praise You for my husband who faithfully trusts in You,

an approved workman who diligently seeks to know

Your will so that he can faithfully walk in it.

Guard him on his path today as He puts action into serving you,

serving his family, and leading others to Christ.

I bind every situation that fights to hinder his faith.

Show him your faithfulness!

JOURNAL PROMPT

What actions will you do unto the Lord?

DAY 16:
A NEW KIND OF GRATEFUL

A grateful heart changed me, and it is about to elevate your entire life...are you ready? Create some space and time away from distraction, time with just the Father. Today is all about putting things into perspective through gratefulness. If you have become downtrodden from something your husband may have said to you, or if you saw life going differently, had a loss, whatever is making it difficult to be grateful; press in to the throne room. If you have focused on a fantasy or dream for your marriage that differs from God's will: give it to Him in PRAYER. Marriage requires a selflessness and purposeful submission. If you thought married life was going make you happier, stare at God's face. (more on Day 23)

If you had planned, hoped, dreamed, prayed, tithed, journaled, fasted, kept chastity, did everything you could for your desired outcome...and you believe that God granted you His will but you can't see the fruit yet, then remain secure in God's big plan. After all, the outcome belongs to Him. Even the promise land requires God to get you through the wilderness first. We can never give from a heart of gratefulness if all we desire is what we cannot attain.

There was a time in my marriage, where it became difficult to even think of one or two things a day to be grateful for. It was because I had become so numb by focusing on what I thought was best, instead of God's best. Gratefulness comes as a steadfast and decisive resolve, no matter if you feel like it's helping. I encourage you to do what I did, and make a change of heart by implementing a new practice.

For 41 days, write a grateful note to your husband. Maybe you won't see an impact at first, but this exercise is about planting seeds into your marriage garden.

Today, stand up in your living room because we are about to use the weapon of a Grateful Heart. When you cannot remember what God has done, you don't want to, or you don't feel like it; if you want to cling to your lack more than what God has done: let His power arise! I know it hurts to not have something you desire. I know it hurts also when you have exited the wilderness, God has provided, and here you are complaining to God that it is still not enough. Lovely daughter, I am here with you. The path to freedom is to flex your gratefulness muscles.

Gratefulness ushers in the peace of Christ. (Colossians 3:15) Gratefulness recalls what exists for your good and praises Jesus for it. Start today by first whipping out the Grateful Heart's buddy, the Praise Weapon. Bear with me as this sounds childlike. I am a firm believer in coming to Jesus with the faith, praise, and relentless joy of a child, a child who doesn't care who watches or judges; she just moves. Get up and move around your living room, as a child, dancing and singing praises of thankfulness unto the Lord. Raise your voice and shout with triumph. God has come to bring you Joy! Begin with no music; just lift your voice. The Lord will come into the room with you and delight in your voice being used for His glory. Gratefulness increases imagination, problem solving, physical health. Gratitude improves psychological health, reduces toxic emotions and depression. Gratitude improves sleep, empathy, self-esteem, and has a major role in overcoming trauma. Cultivate the power of a grateful heart!

LISTEN & WATCH

Psalm 119:103
How sweet are your words to my taste, sweeter than honey to my mouth!

1 Thessalonians 5:18
Give thanks in all circumstances; for this is the will of God in Christ Jesus for you.

Psalm 9:1
I will give thanks to the Lord with my whole heart; I will recount all of your wonderful deeds.

Psalm 95:2
Let us come into His presence with thanksgiving; let us make a joyful noise to Him with songs of praise!

Psalm 147:1
Praise the Lord! For it is good to sing to our God; for it is pleasant, and a song of praise is fitting.

PRAY: *A GRATEFUL PRAISE*

When I cannot hear, unclog my ears;

when I cannot see; unveil my eyes;

when my heart is sick; renew my strength.

Father, I praise You for knowing what I cannot or do not want to

see right now. Forgive me for giving more value to my pain than

freedom in You! I know that You have done and are getting ready

to do exceedingly far beyond what I can pray for or imagine,

so I trust in You. You are my Rock! Your love never fails.

You are Majestic in all Your ways: Your timing, Your answers,

Your promises, Your trials, Your seasons.

I trust your NO and I trust Your YES.

You have never failed me and You won't start now. When I don't

know how to believe this, please open my spirit to see You, to want

You instead of me. I thank you for what You have given me in this

marriage. I thank you for a faithful husband. I thank you for all that

I have because it is great and enough. And anytime I ever think it

isn't in the future, whether that's in five minutes, God I thank you

that You restore Hope. I'll run back to praising and dancing to get

more of Your understanding and fill this Grateful Heart anytime

of the day. You are always worth it. I bless my husband by

my surrender to Jesus. I bring him a full heart; pressed down,

shaken, and running over with thanksgiving.

JOURNAL PROMPT

I am grateful for...

DAY 17:
CONTENTMENT

This was one of the hardest days during my first Prayer Woman fast...but it does not have to be for you, for the Holy Spirit has gone ahead and covered your day. The devotional Jesus gave me for this day is on the character quality of humility. It is the perfect breeding ground for love. Humility is the firm foundation for a strong house that inhabits contentment. If the wife is focused on yesterday's offense, what he did or did not do, how she thought things would be different, then how could contentment reign? Serve one master.

Humility is being in position for serving your husband. You are able to recognize his needs because your interests, needs, desires, wants, identity, energy, and everything about you already exists and is covered, known, found, held, crafted by and flows from Jesus. So, as a Godly wife you are now freely available to pour out generously to him. In this position, selfish ambition is surrendered because a Prayer Woman has already been emptied, satisfied, and fulfilled in Jesus. She is available to respond with grace, instead of react from an empty cup. She is open and not defensive. She offers kindness and joy to her husband. There is no lack in this place of rest with Jesus so there is no need to bring it to your husband. Reread this paragraph until it clicks in your soul.

Don't leave this day until you have completely become emptied in His presence. He will do the work when you ask and invite Him to redefine contentment in your life. You know who you are and whose you are: Jesus knows every intricate detail about your heart, so daughter of the King, you do not need to hold your pain, your lack, or your pride. God's got you! Now that you are feeling more confident in how you can walk in a humble spirit, you are much better prepared to invite contentment into your life. This is not the definition for earthly happiness or a state of satisfaction that comes when you get what you want. This kind of lasting and true contentment is not about a lack of doing or putting up with how things are going as if to keel over and just accept bad apples. On the contrary, the Prayer Woman gains contentment from an inner resolve for keeping her spirit alert, strong, steady, and positioned in Christ. It is being centered in the highs, the lows, grounded in the mountains and in the valleys, in every misfortune, question, and every unexpected conundrum. Whether you face hunger or abundance, destitution or need, you know how to abound in the Spirit! (Philippians 4:12)

When discontentment consumes you, all you feel is a raving hunger for what you do not have. Your mind becomes consumed with what you should have, and you begin to play a narrative that justifies your actions for deserving better. Maybe it feels like you have a promise that is now hurting you. Contentment can still be found, even in the broken places. We live in a fallen world, with the pride of life and lust of the flesh, which is continually at war within our spirit man. But God didn't stop there. Find God's heart, and you'll find contentment. Stay vigilant and attentive. Here is where we live, continually repeating the process for counting it all joy, standing firm in who God says you are, speaking Biblical Truth over yourself, and repenting of pride...so that humility and contentment can co-exist.

LISTEN & WATCH

Philippians 4:11,12
Not that I am speaking of being in need, for I have learned in whatever situation I am to be content. I know how to be brought low, and I know how to abound. In any and every circumstance, I have learned the secret of facing plenty and hunger, abundance and need.

1 Timothy 6:7
Godliness with contentment is great gain.

Luke 12:15
Take care, and be on your guard against all covetousness, for one's life does not consist in the abundance of his possessions.

Ecclesiastes 6:9
Better is the sight of the eyes than the wandering of the appetite: this also is vanity and a striving after wind.

PRAY: *VIGILANT FOR CONTENTMENT*

Lord, take every area of me,

every nook and cranny in my belief systems

about humility, submission, and contentment.

Break down and break off the dispositions that oppose You.

I choose to rest in a spirit of humility.

Contentment is found in You, Father.

My life is no longer my own.

Show me how You provide, Jesus, that as my eyes

become opened up that I may be

filled with gratefulness and great joy.

I lift up my husband,

that he may flourish in Your abounding peace.

May my vigilance for seeking contentment

help him in that peace.

Provide patience for him while I grow in this area.

Bring great contentment for the

valleys and the mountains, that in every season,

our focus remains upon You.

Increase the joy in the contentment for having little,

having nothing, or having much.

Our treasure is in Heaven.

JOURNAL PROMPT

How is contentment is holding you back?

DAY 18:
CAPTURING THOSE THOUGHTS

In 2 Timothy 3, it talks about a person who is constantly weighed down by sins, always learning but never able to come to the knowledge of the truth (vs.6,7). But when you actually have Biblical faith in God's wisdom and instruction, you are fully equipped to endure all persecutions. So, whether that first distraction comes thirty seconds after you wake up or after your cup of morning coffee, it will come. Expect it. The turning point here is deciding ahead of time how you will face it. Will you feed the negative thoughts or claim the promises in the Word? Will you wonder if your husband loves you today and wallow in misery? Pull the reigns, woman!

If your thoughts are not full of life-giving power, then turn to the Word and lean into the power of His joy and His Truth. When you adopt the belief that God's Truth is everything you need to stand firm, then you do! When you adopt the fact that you have been given His joy, instead of relying upon your own, then you have it. You do not need to pray or ask for it daily, you already have access to it as your endless and sufficient resource. Just walk now.

Abstaining from wickedness (2 Timothy 2:19) is to abstain from doubting that you are equipped to fend off temptations, comparison, worry, fear, and the controlling of your own life.

Not fully believing you have already been given the power to walk in victory is holding your own control for your life with closed hands. *Closed hands* = not standing upon His foundation.

The Godly wife and Prayer Woman stands upon the solid Rock of her salvation! She can wisely decipher what is good, noble, pure, and lovely, so that she easily and powerfully walks in her purpose.

When you capture every single thought, you seize God's Joy! Joy is that settled assurance that God is in control; it's the quiet stillness of confidence that everything in Christ will have its way, and it's the determined choice to praise God in every situation. Joy is not a warm feeling or emotion; it is the reward of taking thoughts captive. Take happiness, for example; it is temporary, indicative of a circumstance or a temporary feeling. The Proverbs 31 woman knows the difference of having joy instead of happiness; "she is clothed in strength and dignity and she laughs without fear of the future" (vs.25). In order for her to experience joy, she first binds its opposition: any thought or belief that does not produce fruit. Take thoughts captive when memories come flooding back. Old dreams and memories can replay old battles and make them feel current. But when you capture them, resolve to allow God's transforming power to reign in victory, now and always. Now you are free from repetitive cycles.

Today, you will respond quickly and attentively. You are on guard. You are alert, in charge, and ready to immediately discern what is true and what is a lie. Get into the presence of God to know the difference. If you stay in your mind, the battle will rage on continually. Take authority over your future today.

LISTEN & WATCH

Philippians 4:8
Finally, brothers, whatever is true, whatever is honorable, whatever is just, whatever is pure, whatever is lovely, whatever is commendable, if there is any excellence, if there is anything worthy of praise, think about theses things.

Romans 12:2
Do not be conformed to this world, but be transformed by the renewal of your mind, that by testing you may discern what is the will of God, what is good and acceptable and perfect.

2 Corinthians 10:2
For though we walk in the flesh, we are not waging war according to the flesh. For the weapons of our warfare are not of the flesh but have diving power to destroy strongholds. We destroy arguments and every lofty opinion raised against the knowledge of God, and take every thought captive to obey Christ.

PRAY: *THE DEVIL IS A LIAR*

The devil is a liar. This is not my battle.

Jesus already won it for me.

I cannot wrestle with it or doubt my victory now.

It may look like I am surrounded,

but I am surrounded by You.

This is how I fight my battles.

I was made new. I renew my mind.

I am not going back to be the way I once was, unredeemed,

and unable to take thoughts captive.

The new me is no longer badgered by the old;

I do not even recognize her.

When battles rage, when memories come, when my old

self comes to haunt me and replay itself as if it were alive,

I go ahead and use my weapon:

I open my mouth and speak praises! Praise you Lord!

I praise you for protecting my husband from the enemy.

Show him how to put the devil in his place.

May my husband shine in valiantly in victory.

He is renewed today, standing in victory, knowing his battles, and

walking with discernment to know the difference. Win the battle

in his mind so that he can thrive in the life You created for him;

radiant in the light, full of purity and integrity.

JOURNAL PROMPT

How will Joy help you take your thoughts captive?

DAY 19:
STAND IN NEW GROWTH

There is always an opportunity for new growth. Will you take it? A Prayer Woman seeks, knocks, finds, and stands in new growth. She does not shy away from the trials that bring it forth. Spiritual growth is happening in you right now.

You have made it to Day 19, and I applaud you! You are a rockstar, a shining jewel. The work you are doing on yourself is seen and known by God, and it is commendable. You are a beautiful warrior. I want you to know that God will use your obedience to move your husband. The more you press in to this 41-day journey, the more that God is going to show up! Your diligence to lead yourself and live hidden in Christ, is already another whole level, baby! If you can't feel this joy I have for you, then jump! Yes, go ahead and jump in the air until you feel that rush of joy coming your way.

You've got this because God has got you! The challenges you face for new growth in yourself and for your husband's new growth, is to be expected. Remember, that Jesus never promised there would be difficulty free; He promised that He would always be there for you, that He would answer when you call! The purpose of having the Scriptures right here in the daily prompting is so that you know it is your guide and Jesus will never steer you wrong.

The new growth that is occurring daily for you right now is NEW. You've got to remember that you are on the fast track with God, and that means every single day you change. You are becoming unrecognizable to yourself, your husband, and to those who love you the most. They are not ready for the new you! People will continue to respond, react, and judge you for the way they have already had programmed in their mind for who they think you are because of how you've shown up in the past.

Be aware that your new growth will cause challenges in these relationships. Your testimony is now responding in the new growth while they are still expecting you to react in your old self. Your husband may be caught off guard by your new responses. He may not know how to handle them, and may even become uncomfortable. Expect to get uncomfortable. Pray against resistence and contention.

A Proverbs 31 woman is ready! You are ready and set up for success in Jesus. It will be His success and timing. As you allow Jesus to move in the heart of your husband, you remain on course in that new growth. Even if it causes a disruption in your marriage, pause before you respond and take heart. Tell your spirit to rise up. A disrupt must occur before the new can be birthed. Switch tracks. You may even get sick in bed because you are bearing more self-control than ever, capturing thoughts, dispelling lies, and working your faith muscles in what feels like a marathon.

It's messy at first. But you are showing up, and God is showing out! It might not look like it today, but as I can testify in my own marriage, God has moved my husband over mountains and miles in a short time for what I thought would take years. Be dedicated to your mission, even if you never see the fruit! Your call is Love because Jesus is within you.

LISTEN & WATCH

1 Corinthians 3:6,7
I planted, Apollos watered, but God gave the growth. Neither he who plants nor he who waters is anything, but only God who gives the growth.

John 15:5
I am the vine; You are the branches. Whoever abides in me and I in him, he it is that bears much fruit, for apart from me you can do nothing.

Philippians 1:21
For to me to live is Christ, and to die is gain.

Proverbs 1:7
The fear of the Lord is the beginning of knowledge; fools despise wisdom and instruction.

Psalm 91:1
He who dwells in the shelter of the Most High will abide in the shadow of the Almighty.

PRAY: *CALL OF GROWTH*

When I cannot see how, I believe.

When I am rapidly shifting and wading through uncharted

territory because of this new growth, my spirit is calm in

Your presence. The Lord never leaves me. He knows my mission,

and the price I am paying to get there. Jesus, carry my burden,

because I am on mission for my new growth to bless my

husband. My new growth will uproot and disrupt evil cycles.

As I dispel darkness by walking in growth,

I know that You will sustain me in my frailty.

Speak to me in the darkest moments of my shift.

Cover my husband with love, while I am still learning

to walk in the footprints after my Daddy.

Provide for him the grace to understand.

Keep his spirit and mind open to viewing me with new eyes.

Move upon his heart, even now, for the shift.

May my growth even inspire his new growth.

Keep him close to Your heart, guarded from the

attacks and lies of the enemy.

As I abide in You, Abba, I know that You are on the

move in my husband; to protect him, love him, lead,

cover, guide, and move in him,

because he is Your precious son.

JOURNAL PROMPT

Ask God to keep you close, so He can remove weariness.

DAY 20:
PERSEVERANCE

Keep stepping, woman. SAY YES TO JESUS!

When you have this much new growth budding in your garden, you cannot help but look differently than from when you began. As the bud comes forth, it expands in size. It needs more space as it matures and yields its tending to the Gardener. For a seed to germinate and not rot, it must first undergo a process of drying out in direct sunlight for a period of time. Drying out hardens and seals the protective coat around the inner parts. If that seed is planted prematurely or without being dried, the seed will rot and suffer from attacks like disease or pests.

Darling, you are this seed. You are undergoing the direct heat in this prayer journey *so that* you can be planted and take root!

What happens when we resist the heat? We resist the pressure required to come into our fullest potential. We wilt, get overtaken, and never get to bloom. But you have a choice: to withstand the pressure and heat in order to develop, or not. Jesus will never force His will upon you. Instead, He provides opportunity for you to accept it. What happens if we do not secure enough time with Jesus as our sun? We begin to decay: we act selfish, angry, rude, short, and unkind. When pride clouds our spirit man, our vision becomes unclear for what Jesus is really producing.

It takes perseverance! Daughter of God, here is your exhortation to keep on stepping, no matter how difficult the path is ahead. Your perseverance in your YES is the beginning of the power needed for your next level of spiritual maturity.

Your YES to Jesus will cause you to become unrecognizable to whom you were before! Only dipping one toe in to the pool will never cause the shift you are in need of; you have to jump all the way in, and stay there with great determination and perseverance.

No matter the cost will become your mantra. Yes, even when your family shuns you, even when you lose friendships. The place that God is taking you is vastly different than where your previous version could go. Nobody is ready for the new you, but they need the healed you.

Today, you will run this race, both feet in, all the way, no matter what you face. Wife, Prayer Woman, you know the God who saves, the God who holds your heart. He will never fail you in your move-ment towards Him. When you detach from where you were and are, to answer His will for your life, it takes 100% abandonment to everything that was: your beliefs about yourself, your way of doing things, your way of thinking, your friends, your family. Persevere into the path God is setting before you. Out of the old and into the new. Rise up, warrior, and take your place. Push through the muck. Wade through the deep waters. Go where you have never been. Do what God is leading you to do. Forge new pathways. Blaze new trails. Go through the doors where God gives you the keys. Take the territory for His glory. You can't do all of this if you stay stuck, silent, and the same.

It gets lonely in the season of transformation, when you are dried in that heat, but you are about to be planted so that you may bloom in a Garden, mastered by Jesus! Woman, evolve.

LISTEN & WATCH

Isaiah 26:3
You keep him in perfect peace whose mind is stayed on you, because he trusts in you.

Romans 5:3,4
...We rejoice in our sufferings, knowing that suffering produces endurance, and endurance produces character, and character produces hope, and hope does not put us to shame, because God's love has been poured into our hearts through the Holy Spirit who has been given to us.

1 Corinthians 3:9,13-15
For we are God's fellow workers; you are God's field, you are God's building...each one's work will become clear; for the Day will declare it, because it will be revealed by fire; and the fire will test each one's work, of what sort it is...if anyone's work is burned up, he will suffer loss, though he himself will be saved, but only as through fire.

PRAY: *LONELY IN THE HEAT*

Father, today, I embrace the heat. My answer is a resounding and emphatic YES to obeying Your will for my life and my marriage.

My life is Yours. This marriage is Yours, and as the King who holds it all together, lead me and provide the spiritual strength to endure with perseverance. I know that through this deeper level of perseverance, You have something awesome planned to show me. As I wait, I stand in faith, believing that where you are leading me is safe, good, powerful, and beautiful. Thank you for going ahead of me to craft what is on the other side of what I can only see as difficult and seemingly impossible.

I serve a Great God and You are trustworthy.

I count Your promises daily. As I walk in this heat, I know that I am becoming a new woman, so thank you for watching over me.

Hide me in the shadow of Your wings.

Open my husband's spiritual eyes to trust and praise that it's You doing the work in my transformation.

Shelter him in the understanding of You growing in me, that the cost of this birthing process is for his blessing, not his demise.

May the Holy Spirit increase within my husband to bring attentiveness to Your voice and Your inner work. Increase his muscles of discernment and attentiveness to the Holy Spirit. Knit us together as one, deeper than all of our yesterdays.

JOURNAL PROMPT

What area of loneliness are you giving to Jesus today?

DAY 21:
FORGIVENESS

Day 21! Woman, you are on FIRE!!!

I applaud your diligence in this journey. Remember, that your deep, inner work to BECOME the woman who first & continually runs to fill her well at Jesus' feet, in prayer, is the woman God's ear is leaned down to hear. He is near.

Your appetite is growing...if you started this journal, barely glancing at one or two verses, you may have your Bible or Bible app actually open in front of you now, pouring over the verses. At first, it probably felt like drinking from a waterfall, but now your thirst has grown to: 'I can't get enough, I need more, I crave more, I need more of Jesus than I did before!'

The challenges that are surfacing in your marriage this week are because Jesus is uprooting sin and wiping it away. He is at work. It feels like it gets worse before it gets better because everything that God is removing, surfaces: it's now uprooted and floating right in front of you, all stinky and bigger than life. But wisdom says that if you adopt the perspective of Jesus, from where He is standing, above your situation, that sin is no more. To you, it's all you can see. So, put on your dancing shoes and drink from His well of living water. I wrote down those Scripture verses to lead you into a thirst, for your well to be filled, your miracles to arrive, and your heart to have hope again.

Prayer Woman, you are arriving at a place of prayer for your husband, where you truly believe that prayer is your lifestyle;

not a temporary add-on. It is your weapon for life and death. Picture what it means to BE alive in your spiritual lens, looking at Jesus: He is the Way, the Truth, and the Life. Jesus is Life. Your forgiveness is life. The power of your tongue has life and death in it.

Wife, your forgiveness to your husband, unleashes the force of a giant slayer at the devil. It yields the sword of destruction to the blockage that the devil desires to divide you two. You are a Prayer Woman, and you are awake to anything and everything that causes division. Ask you seek Him, God will develop a spiritual maturity in you for this. You are rocking this out!

Following Christ is about partnering with God's will and God's promises for his heirs to His Kingdom, not storing religion as head knowledge. Following Him is not a formula; it's a personal relationship with a Father who went first. He showed us how to forgive, so that we can forgive. He is our perfect example and He is the power behind our weapon of forgiveness. In aligning yourself with what Christ did on the cross, you wield His power, which breaks chains, heals, binds, and delivers.

You picked up this journal to pray over your husband, to fight for unity: this is how you do it! Forgive him. Forgive his present and his future. Yes, and definitely forgive his past. Forgive all the people in his past. Draw the line in the sand for him so that no past sin, soul ties, brokenness, unforgiveness, pain, sorrow, cycles, nothing can come into the covenant he has with you. You are the warrior who battles with him and for him. You are letting the devil know who is boss; there's a prayer woman in town and nothing passes her: only LOVE, grace, and blessing grow here.

LISTEN & WATCH

Ephesians 4:32
Be kind to one another, tenderhearted, forgiving one another, as God in Christ forgave you.

Colossians 3:12,13,14
Put on then, as God's chosen ones, holy and beloved, compassionate hearts, kindness, humility, meekness, and patience, bearing with one another and, if one has a complaint against another, forgiving each other; as the Lord has forgiven you, so you also must forgive. And above all these put on love, which binds everything together in perfect harmony.

Ephesians 4:31
Let all bitterness and wrath and anger and clamor and slander be put away from you, along with all malice.

Matthew 18:22
Jesus said to him, "I do not say to you seven times, but seventy-seven times."

PRAY: *FORGIVENESS*

Lord, I forgive every person who has sinned against my husband. I forgive every woman who has ever mistreated him, broken him, caused him pain & sinned against him. I forgive every person who has done him wrong, spread lies, done evil and caused division in their heart against him. I cancel every force of evil. I bind lust, envy, & greed. I break the strongholds of fear, pride, victimhood, and anything that has pummeled him to the ground. I say "GET UP, HUSBAND! GOD IS NOT DONE WITH YOU YET. HE HAS ONLY JUST BEGUN!

You may have been forsaken, wronged, accused, forgotten, abused, spat on, rejected, and cast out, but this Prayer Woman, YOUR WIFE, is ON MISSION to behead the devil by using her Weapon of Forgiveness."

Husband, you are covered by my prayers. God is your head and you are my head in this marriage. YOU are wildly protected from all harm. I protect you from even my own sinful nature by submitting to the Lord. May our enemies become so troubled in their schemes to injure and divide us that they cease and turn to You, Jesus. You are full of forgiveness.

I thank you for setting my husband and I upon solid ground. Wherever we walk, the favor of the Lord keeps us. People who adhere to the lies of the devil may run us out of a building, but no one can remove us from the POSITION that Jesus gave us.

JOURNAL PROMPT

What areas do you need to forgive your husband?

DAY 22:
GO TO BATTLE, WARRIOR QUEEN

From ash to beauty, you are rising! Jesus is the ultimate example for leading a life as a Godly woman. As God wars for you, you war for your husband. As God breaks the chains off of you, your prayer is used as a weapon for Jesus to break your husband's chains. Your faith, your intercession, and your purity rises as sweet aroma to the King of Heaven. Prayer is your weapon. Your mouth is your weapon. Go ahead and use it!

You are in a spiritual battle for your man right now. Queen, you have purposefully arrived on day 22 by forging a new path in your life. Don't give up! Don't get weary. Look to the ant, as it meticulously and tirelessly works. Awaken from the slumber of avoiding prayer, where poverty comes like a thief in the night to rob what is yours. Don't allow what Father has bestowed upon you for stewardship to be stolen. As a Warrior Queen, your purpose is to walk in God's strength: spiritual, physical, mental, emotional. When your spiritual strength is first fed from being in the presence of God; it aligns the rest.

Remember, you are in a battle that has already been won in Heaven for you. It is your position to pull it down and usher it forth for your husband; and that's done by prayer.

Ask, Seek, Knock! Open your mouth, be wise, be slow to anger. Walk in the fruit of the spirit by being led by the Holy Spirit.

THIS IS HOW YOU WAR, QUEEN!

Queen Esther used her position with great poise, grace, patience, and wisdom. Before Esther did anything, she first recognized what battle existed, gathered the information, gathered her people, her ladies, and family for fasting. Get connected. Get linked up with women who know the Word of God and who will war beside you.

Esther called a fast! Why? Because she knew that strategy is the first order of business for winning a battle. It was only then that she waited three nights of dining the King before she opened her mouth to gain the king's favor. She knew patience and she had the wisdom to war for her people from it.

In Esther 5:1 it says, "On the third day, Esther put on her royal robes and stood in the inner court of the king's palace...and when the king saw her standing in the court, she won favor in his sight, and he held out the golden scepter." The story continues with the king asking what Esther's request was and he immediately granted it to her...and he gave her half the kingdom. WOW, the overflow!

Woman of God, you are this warrior queen, poised, calm, collected, knowing how to get your spirit right before the Lord. Strategize: go to prayer and fasting first. Get your anointed, God-fearing ladies rallied in prayer before you ever go to your husband for your request. If you read that passage in Esther, you will notice how all she then did is stand in the court and the king's heart had already moved to 'whatever you desire'. As a wife, it is not your role to complain, change, teach, nag, convince, or control our husband. Nor is it your place to gossip to people about how awful your husband is. Instead, by linking arms with prayerful women, we usher forth faith and activate God's authority.

LISTEN & WATCH

Proverbs 6:6-8
Go to the ant, Oh sluggard; consider her ways, and be wise.
Without having any chief, officer, or ruler, she prepares her bread
in summer and gathers her food in harvest.

1 Peter 3:3
Do not let your adorning be external - the braiding of the hair and
the putting on of gold jewelry, or the clothing you wear - but let
your adorning be the hidden person of the heart with the imperishable beauty of a gentle and quiet spirit, which in God's sight is very
precious.

Ephesians 4:11-14
And he gave the apostles, the prophets, the evangelists, the shep-
herds and teachers, to equip the saints for the work of ministry, for
building up the body of Christ, until we all attain to the unity of the
faith and of the knowledge of the Son of God, to mature manhood,
to the measure of the stature of the fullness of Christ, so that we
may no longer be children, tossed to and fro by the waves and
carried about by every wind of doctrine, but human cunning, by
craftiness in deceitful schemes.

PRAY: *GETTING PREPARED*

I come to You, today, with an open and yielded heart,

on mission to being prepared as the Queen of this home.

I first recognize that I AM THE HOME. From my time with

Jesus, flow miracles into my family. I get ready!

I set my gaze upon being in the presence of the Lord,

linking arms with my fellow prayer warrior ladies, & taking the

time I need to wait upon the Lord. I give You my time, my mouth,

my praise. I begin my battle right here, in the quiet space of my

spirit. As a Prayer Woman, I don't move first. I get prepared.

I get still. I PUT ON the royal robes of prayer and fasting.

I equip myself with the armor of God as I shed what I want

for personal gain. Just as Queen Esther valiantly presented herself,

she did so with this set in her heart: 'if it pleases my husband', 'I go

even if it means dying', which was the opposite of getting her way,

getting her people free. Lord, give me this kind of

heart towards You, Jesus, and for my husband.

Show me this kind of power in submission.

Go before me and begin to open my husband's eyes for me, as

only You can do. I would fail on my own, but in You, I trust that

no matter the circumstance, no matter the outcome,

You know my heart and I am at peace with Your way.

Minister to my husband a spirit of compassion,

receptiveness, deference, and love.

JOURNAL PROMPT

How will you prepare as a Prayer Warrior Queen?

DAY 23:
STARE AT GOD'S FACE

When life feels good...or when life is broken...
When life is busy...or when life is lonely...
When life is full...or when life has no answers...
STARE AT GOD'S FACE!

The mistake that a lot of couples make is too little of time spent staring at God, and way too much time lost staring at each other. God's design for marriage isn't that our spouse fulfills us, but that because of the unity for a mission bigger than the two of us, God is glorified. Grow your discipline for seeking God's face, and the rest will fall away. Ponder the angels: (Revelation 4), they sing 'Holy, holy holy is the Lord God Almighty', continually, for all of eternity. Seek the Lord and dwell in His house. Gaze upon the beauty of the Lord (Psalm 27:4). This is your answer to any problem.

Your life on earth, as a wife, is for just a short and temporary time. When you shift your focus onto eternity, you will develop a burning desire to just be with Abba. Your need will be taken care of in the background, as you close your eyes and gaze upon Him for who He is. Right now, He sees you. Just by practicing this worship regularly, many of your problems will disappear in your marriage. It definitely did for mine, because marriage problems aren't really marriage problems; they are God problems. Be in Him. Rest in Him. Praise Him.

The more we stare at God's face, the more we operate in who He intends us to be. If we stop placing God at the center of our lives, then we begin to operate in the brokeness, and our Godly mission becomes compromised. So, start playing big and lean in to Jesus. The unhealed version of you is the immature, needy, and selfish one. Stare at becoming made in the image of God instead of in the image of yourself. Here is where you can show up with Godly maturity, because He heals you in His presence. An healed you brings blessing, glory, and honor in everything you touch. You will only be able to see and have God's perfect will inside the Garden of your marriage if you are a woman who places her spiritual walk above everything else. If we pick up pride, self-ishness, or self-serving behavior, which is outside His will for us, then we are allowing the flesh to blind us from seeing His will.

When we pick up ungodliness and impurity it blinds us from obtaining the available fruit. We, then, operate in a version of ourselves that was never meant for a marriage grounded in God. That means that no amount of working out an issue with our husband, in and of ourselves, without seeking Jesus first, will ever arrive to a peaceful, Godly conclusion. Sin and spiritual fruit just don't match.

The more we stare at God's face, the more our spirit rises up and we can operate from the renewing of the mind, redemption, grace, patience, holiness, and purity. This is our promised portion inside His will for our marriage. If we reside outside of it we don't get the fullness of all that He intended the garden of marriage to be. We cut Him short and idolize our control. God made marriage work if we put Jesus first. So, if we are in the Garden, we must live according to its original design. Begin, today, to live fully alive in setting the atmoshere for His glory!

LISTEN & WATCH

Proverbs 14:27
The fear of the Lord is a fountain of life, that one may turn away from the snares of death.

1 John 4:13,16,18
By this we know that we abide in Him and He in us, because He has given us of His Spirit.

We have come to know and to believe the love that God has for us. God is love, and whoever abides in God, and God abides in him.

There is no fear in love, but perfect love casts out fear. For fear has to do with punishment, and whoever fears has not been perfected in love.

Ecclesiastes 5:2b
God is in Heaven and you are on earth. Therefore, let your words be few.

PRAY: *REVERE GOD*

God, I revere you. I run into Your presence just to be near You.

Grow my desire to stare at Your face. I am here, praying,

because I long to increase my intimacy with You. Help me

to bring my heart before my need. Help me to long for sitting at

Your feet and being still. You are a Great God and I revere You.

You are Glorious and Praiseworthy.

You are the God of the heavens and the earth,

so my words are few today as I take this time to be in awe of You.

Perfect me in love so that I may love You more and be

Your agape love to my husband.

Your will, Your power, Your answers, God.

For my husband, woo him to spend more time with You,

to sit at your feet, shut off the world and breathe You into his being.

I pray that You would orchestrate his day where things get

cancelled or go more swiftly; clear paths, so that He has more

time being in love with You. Speak to His spirit and draw him

closer to You. Even now, awaken him from the inside to answer

the unction of the Spirit so that he meets You in his car, in his

thoughts, in his radio; show up for him. I bless Your name for

giving me a husband who places You first; I believe this in faith

and I testify daily that it is so, and set course to admonish him in it.

JOURNAL PROMPT

How can you revere God today? Pour out your heart.

DAY 24:
ALL NEW

The transformation of growth for unity, peace, harmony, and more of God's fruit in your marriage begins with YOU; it begins with a *new* you. During this journey through these 41 days, you have committed yourself to becoming a new you, _____.

I wish I knew your name, so that I could pen it in the blank above. Beloved daughter of God, this is written with you in mind: to the wife, to the daughter, to the mom, to the single woman, to the empty nester, to the widow, to the teenager, to the grandmother, to the aunt, to the WOMAN out there looking for her miracle.

It begins with the ALL NEW you, strong woman.

You are the clay and He is the Potter. He is molding and forming you. Sometimes our heart gets hard and we have to break open and become 'cleansed' again in order take on our new form. The transformation is a process; it's a journey of trust. Our hearts change, our minds become clear, we become unrecognizable as a blob of clay before we become the completed masterpiece. When life brings hardship we might fall and crack or shatter. But it's not your ending.

God gave me a prophetic dream more than a decade ago where I was a crystal vase sitting on the top shelf of a glass showroom. The fluorescent lighting was brightly shining through the ornate etchings of my glass.

I was on the top shelf because I was special to my creator. Then, something wobbled nearby and the vase crashed to the ground. I was now on the floor in nearly a thousand pieces, thinking "I'll never look new or beautiful again". But then the glass shop owner gathered up every single shard and jagged piece of me, put me into a leather bag and carried me to the workshop. It took time; it took years. But while he worked on me, he gently and firmly whispered "I am putting every piece back in the same place to where it was before because I created you perfectly, and this time in between every broken piece you will be held together by my special kind of resin. As the new you, I will install a new light directly above you to shine down through the inside of your vase so that the light shines through the clear resin and casts a prism. This is your reminder that I am your adhesive, your creator, your light, and you will never go a day again without feeling me in between every piece of you."

I share this today because it is such a beautiful story of how God does the same thing with us when we get broken. Jesus picks up all of our pieces *to* put them back together, but we don't look the same. We have scars to remind us that our story and our purpose was not over yet when we broke. He then gives us new purpose in our all new look. Now, with more of God holding together all of my brokenness, I am expanded to hold more.

More weight, more glory.
The more we let go of how we think we need to be shaped and just allow the Potter to form us, the more beautiful we become. He takes our battle wounds, our ashes, our broken pain and makes us beautiful, full of power and purpose again. Lean in to your new beauty, woman of powerful position!

LISTEN & WATCH

2 Corinthians 5:17
Therefore, if anyone is in Christ, he is a new creation. The old has passed away; behold, the new has come.

Psalm 51:8,12
Let me hear joy and gladness; let the bones that you have broken rejoice. Restore me to the joy of your salvation, and uphold me with a willing spirit.

Psalm 51:17
The sacrifices of God are a broken spirit; a broken and contrite heart, O God, you will not despise.

Isaiah 41:10
Fear not, for I am with you; be not dismayed, for I am Your God; I will strengthen you, I will help you, I will uphold you with my righteous right hand.

Joel 2:25
I will restore to you the years that the swarming locust has eaten, the hopper, the destroyer, and the cutter, my great army...

PRAY: *NEW*

Lord, I don't pretend to know *how* You mend me, but I feel
You every time You are at work. I know that no matter what
has happened to me in the past or what is happening right now,
that Your steadfast love grants life to me.
Your care preserves my spirit. Sometimes You hide these in
Your heart from me, until I am ready, until I make a move,
but I know that this is your purpose. (Job 10:7-13)
Protect the all new me from old ways, old habits,
old places I used to go that no longer serve my new growth.
Give me great Godfidence to stand on mission for ushering
Your glory. Help me depart from things that You no longer want
in my life: certain people, community, how my time is spent,
and where I spend money. Give me discernment to pivot and
cut off any and all on your list.
I pray over my husband's mind: guard him from what is
no longer part of his life, keep him in humility, and open his eyes
to the things You need him to shed before his next level up.
My prayer for him today is that he is shielded in his new beauty.
God, I've seen You moving in my husband, and I ask for
protection over that new growth. I bind the attack of the enemy
and the people and temptations that the devil uses to get my
husband off track. I praise You, Father, for my husband is a
triumphant warrior who keeps his gaze upon You!

JOURNAL PROMPT

Your 3 new growth areas from the past 24 days are:

DAY 25:
OPT IN

Hello dear sister! You are called and appointed for this day. Jesus has already been crafting your resources and unlocking doors for you to step with Him today. Grab onto His hand and this prayer book to stir up and dig in to your victory!

Here is my story of God's provision:
I am sitting here at my kitchen table, writing the pages of this book, pouring out every word from a soul that's been transformed because Jesus has used my mess for His glory. I've been writing for a few days now, only emptying out the words that the Holy Spirit allows me. Today I began to feel very ill. I laid down for a twenty-minute nap, and awoke to my oldest son smiling at me, telling me in the kindest voice you have ever heard, "Wake up, Mommy. It's time to write God's book." He strokes my shoulder and holds my hand, and then I look up at his face and it is glowing! Pure radiant beams from his eyes peer down at me and he begins to pray over me: "Jesus, may Mommy walk in the seven fruits of the spirit, and every word she writes be from You. Heal her and give her all that she needs to obey. Amen." If you are not sobbing yet, just wait. I walk downstairs and lay on my husband, legs curled up on his lap, head on shoulder. I am shuddering as if to break out in a high fever. My body is completely shutting down. My husband smiles at me and says, "if you need to rest, go sleep, and I'll take care of the kids, but if you have any strength, use it to write." I feel his strength and decide to get up and walk over to the kitchen table to write. The words begin to pour out more rapidly than any other day I have sat to write. Within 40 minutes, I look up and the Holy Spirit whispers,

"how do you feel?" I hold my head in my cupped hands, weeping. "I feel AMAZING!" All of a sudden, I realize I am not sick anymore, but God has empowered me with supernatural energy!

I share this story today because it is a testimony of OPTING IN! The opt in was for me to decide to continue being obedient, to get it done by the date Jesus told me was His publishing day for this book. I have had unbelievable hurdles, but Jesus has always provided the way through. That's His promise.

Jesus will always provide your way to OPT IN to Him. No matter how tired, sick, in pain, or out of money, He is the way. Whether the kids are loud, the husband walks out on you, you get taken to court, you go bankrupt, you lose a baby, your house burns down, you become deathly ill...let me ask you: *how much do you crave JESUS?*

I know the God of the impossible, the unfortunate, the broken, the lost, the "way too far gone". I know a God who is in the same room as you are, and He is ready, available, and holding all of the power. All you need to do is just say 'yes!' You can't see it right now, but your provision is on the other side of your opt in! Push through the pain, for He is your Miracle Maker! May God keep growing your provisions right in front of you. Awaken to see them.

Woman, let me hear you roar your

Y

E

S

!!!

LISTEN & WATCH

2 Corinthians 1:20
For all the promises of God find their YES in him. That is why it is through Him that we utter our Amen to God for His glory.
Psalm 84:2
My soul longs, yes, even faints for the courts of the Lord; my heart and flesh sing for joy to the living God.
Psalm 85:12
Yes, the Lord will give what is good, and our land will yield its increase.
Psalm 90:17a
Let the favor of the Lord our God be upon us, and establish the work of our hands upon us.
John 5:8
Jesus said to him, "Get up, take up your bed, and walk."
NOTE: this man had to first get up, then God provided his healing.

PRAY: *MY OPT IN FOR MY MIRACLE*

Lord, I put on my shield of faith, which is to know that You are strong when I am weak. I praise You for the miracles that are chasing after me. My opt in, Lord, is choosing to not to pick up hurt, but to instead, respond from the energy and spiritual fruit that comes by abiding in You. My opt in is when I choose to give grace and meekness even when I want to get irritated. My opt in for my marriage's unity is when I run to my knees and get still before You, God! My opt in is to never give up on your promises.

When I don't know where to turn or how to change anything, when the pain is too much to carry, when my burden isn't light, I run to the living well of Jesus' presence. Your yoke is easy and Your burden is light, so I lay at Your feet. I know that my victory is on its way. It's already made available for me in the heavens. My opt in is surrender, submission, praise, and faith. I call forth my miracle. Lord hasten quickly to my plea, and fill me with Your peace and gratitude until it arrives. Secure his heart and mind in faith, to believe for it, to know it is on its way and praise You in the storm as though the miracles were already here. Give my husband great fortitude in his mind, to surrender to the call upon his life, to surrender to Jesus, serve his wife, disciple his family, and give generously to others. Bless Your name for the husband I get to serve alongside everyday for building the Kingdom of God.

JOURNAL PROMPT

How can you opt in for Jesus to bring your miracle today?

DAY 26:
GOD ANSWERS FERVENCY

The fervent prayers of a righteous woman produces wonderful results. This is a beautiful promise. Prayer Woman, your prayers have great power. In the Bible, it says prayer with faith will save the one who is sick (James 5:15), and that the Lord will raise him up. If you need it to rain (vs.17) in your marriage, pray. Let it rain perfect love which casts out fear. Let it rain unity! Amen! If it does not happen right away, pray again, pray fervently. Pray without ceasing. Praise as if it is already completed in the heavens for you. Pray in faith, believing that even if you never see it happen in your lifetime, that it will come to pass. We must pray without selfish ambition, but with generosity.

To be fervent in spirit is to be full of zeal for the Lord.

Fervency in faith extinguishes the fiery darts of the evil one (Ephesians 6:16); it moves him under your feet, as you are alert with perseverance, boldly declaring the mystery of the Gospel. This 41-day fast is developing a course of fervency in your life as a *lifestyle*. It's not just for these forty-one days; this is just the beginning. It is forging the path for healing in your life, which then flows into your husband's life, and to your entire household. The Prayer Woman looks well to the ways of her household, yes, but she does so first by filling her own well, earnestly and diligently seeking the Lord's face.

Seeking God first changes you, which then gives you the keys to boldly cultivate the presence of God in your home. When you spend time with ABBA, the atmosphere shifts in you. You become full. You spill over. What develops in you fills the rooms in your house, your office, your car, your church, your neighborhood, and beyond.

You set the Living Aura® for the home because you are a woman who is fervently abiding in the power of Jesus. It is not about striving and trying anymore. It is *becoming* and *being* known in the fervency, not in the doing more. This kind of presence moves people and situations. Watch, as your husband comes home, walks through the door, and within minutes you see his whole countenance begin to glow with joy and peace. Watch, as your child snaps out of bad behavior because his spirit gets nurtured and aligned. Watch, as your health recovers, your peace restores, your hope renews, and your marriage flourishes!

After all, life is much more about Jesus than it is about you, so when you cannot believe how Jesus will do it, remember that He is the God who made everything from nothing. You do not have to be perfect because Jesus' power is made perfect in your weakness. Behavior gets refined from first setting God as the foundation of your fervency. He is the Great Shepherd to guide you and be your Master Teacher. So, you see, there is nothing to fear anymore. You are amazing. You are safe, known, and fully held in your journey.

I love how 1 Peter 3 reveals the eight virtues that should characterize believers who follow Christ. Verses 8-9: we have sublime harmony, brotherly love, sympathy, kindness, humility, fervent love, no retaliation, and we speak blessings on those who mistreat us. If you want to embrace true life and find beauty in each day, stop speaking evil. Instead, cultivate an eager pursuit of peace. God sees this. And His heart responds (1 Peter 3:12).

LISTEN & WATCH

Romans 12:11,12
Do not be slothful in zeal, be fervent in spirit, serve the Lord.
Rejoice in hope, be patient in tribulation, be constant in prayer.
2 Corinthians 12:9
My grace is sufficient for you, my power is made perfect in
weakness.
James 1:4
Let steadfastness have its full effect, that you may be perfect and
complete, lacking in nothing.
1 Peter 4:8
Above all, keep loving one another earnestly, since love covers a
multitude of sins.
James 5:17,18
Elijah was a man with a nature Ike ours, and he prayed fervently
that is might not rain, and for three years and six months it did not
rain on the eart. They he prayed again, and heaven gave raiin, and
the earth bore its fruit.

PRAY: *MY PRAYER HAS GREAT POWER*

I earnestly seek You, ABBA, so that only You are seen in all of me. I long for You because I desire to show You to my family and my husband; that by sowing Jesus into them, we might become perfected in Love. You are the God who forges the path ahead of me. You know where I am going and how I will get there, because I commit to doing it Your way. Teach me how to pray and how to live in a way that doesn't limit You. As I live this prayer life as a lifestyle, be my source, be my guide. Be the reason for the tone I set in my household. Be the Living Aura® in me so that I can set the atmosphere and tone. May it flow from fervently abiding in Your presence. Fill grace in my speech. May I be meek and bold.

Set me ablaze in my powerful purpose to fervently pray. Ignite my husband. Light him up just from getting close to my flames, because I've taken a seat at Your fireplace. Light up our home from the way we usher in Jesus, the way we communicate, exhort, encourage, and pray for each other. I fervently seek You God, to be the overflow in me. May Your Spirit walk the halls in my house. Run through the floors and up the walls. Keep the window cracks sealed from the enemy, that the fire on the inside of me would set my whole household on fire for You, Jesus! It starts with me. It starts here, in my fervent prayers.

Ignite unity!

JOURNAL PROMPT

My fervent prayers for my heart & my husband's heart:

DAY 27:
STEWARDSHIP & STOREHOUSES

Daughter of God, how do you fill your cup, your spiritual storehouse for being able to pour out, give unending, and act like Jesus in your marriage?

Fuel your storehouse by spending time with the Creator of those resources. God is faithful to provide all that you need: forgiveness, a fresh daily start, hope, and so many more amazing promises. Do not allow them to fade, run out, or become overshadowed. You were set on mission as a Wife for such a time as this, with great power in your purpose. But it's not your power. It's not what you try so hard to do right all in your own might. Are you ready to rewrite your past story? Gone are the days of your well drying up because it wasn't watered by the presence of the Holy Spirit. Come alive and flourish in Him. Sure, it may feel easier to take control of all your effort, but your humanity limits you and does not produce the life-giving fruit you were designed to yield.

If you are not fully awakened to living by the Holy Spirit, your well runs dry. Since the moment you gave your life to Jesus, you relinquished this control. You made a commitment to do life Jesus' way, instead of your own. This path has many hardships and times of wilderness; to test you, to show your need for Him, and most importantly, to give you opportunity to love Jesus more.

He is crazy about you! His infinite love is the deep well. Prayer Woman, recognize your vital responsibility to steward your spirit well. If you're running low on abiding in Him, what happens?

You get tired, you focus on desire, you compare. Maybe you have picked up complaining and even control. It's a slippery slope at that point. Feed the flesh, and you'll get more flesh. If you don't get back to filling your storehouse with Jesus, then uncontrollable desire turns into envy, covetousness, and bitterness. These spirits are not of God. They are set out to destroy your Godly spirit.

Those evil spirits want to take advantage of the gap or crack that occurred between operating in God's spirit and picking up the flesh. You know, that time when your husband said something vexing and you had a split second to decide if you would pick it up and feed it; if you would allow it to disturb your spirit or not. This is the moment where the Prayer Woman must be alert. She sees it, she gets collected within, and prays *"God, hold this for me because it's too much to handle. Hold all the parts of me so that I don't use them to react in an ungodly way towards my husband. Now, grant me the courage to stand in complete peace as I generously give to him from You."* Read those words carefully; the ones that say *give to him from You,* **not of me**.

The power, lovely wife, is in a solid stance where she lets God hold her heart so that she no longer is in a position of defense or lack. Yes, even while he may be dishing out his own pride. His behavior does not determine your respect. You can no longer react in sin because you gave Jesus all of you first! You became emptied out of you at the feet of Jesus, and full of only God's strength. Do you feel this power? Yes woman! You've got this. This is another part of the "opt in" from Day 25. Keep building the storehouse and shedding what doesn't belong. Make God be the Lord of your life. Your marriage will follow suit.

LISTEN & WATCH

Joshua 1:6
Be strong and courageous, for you shall cause this people to inherit the land that I swore to their fathers to give them.

Proverbs 6:16-19
There are six things that the Lord hates, seven that are an abomination to him: haughty eyes, a lying tongue, and hands that shed innocent blood, a heart that devises wicked plans, feet that make haste to run to evil, a false witness that breathes out lies, and the one who sows discord among brothers.

Psalm 119:105
Your Word is a lamp to my feet and a light to my path.

Ephesians 6:10
Finally, be strong in the Lord and in the strength of His might.

PRAY: *BE STRONG*

Lord, I take courage in Your strength. I run to Your arms, for

You are my refuge and strong tower. In You alone, I am made

strong. Here is where I live: in Your presence.

I am joyfully running to be with the One whom I love,

my Father, my Rock, my Salvation, and my Defender.

Come be all that You are, in my heart, in my mind, & in my words.

Hold my plans, home, business, marriage, family; all of this is not

mine for there is no more of my will apart from You, Lord.

Today, and forevermore, You are King!

Come fill my spirit to overflowing, that I may minister to my

husband from this spring of living water.

Fill him with You, Jesus. I commit to pausing and waiting before

speaking, before responding; that my response may come from

being held in Jesus, not by my flesh. If it is of me, I'll hold it

wrong and see pain or make pain. On my own, I cannot omit

defensiveness or pride. So, teach me to be a steward who fills her

storehouse from Jesus, so that I can be a blessing to my husband.

No matter what I think is stolen from me or thrown at me, I won't

pick it up. My peace is hidden in You, and in return, it blesses and

ministers peace to my husband. I choose to bless my husband with

this peace. He thrives in Jesus and his storehouses are busting

open with the Goodness of the Lord.

JOURNAL PROMPT

How can I be a better steward today?

DAY 28:
INTENTIONAL

Prayer Woman, you are already being so intentional about digging in to these pages everyday. Be very proud of your hard work. Hang in there and keep your commitment to your fast, because the road ahead for the next thirteen days will be revolutionary!

As a Godly wife, there is a lot to be intentional about:
intentional **gratitude**,
intentional **prayer**,
intentional **praise**,
intentional **stance**,
intentional **generosity**,
intentional **warring**.
You are pressing deeper and uncovering a courageous spirit and discipline that you will use for the rest of your life.

Intentionality in prayer drives movement in the Spirit.
Prayer unlocks closed spaces.

You are now living in the space where courage matures in you from the heart of God. It lives in hope. All you do is open your life and invite it inside. When you cannot feel hope or be hopeful, just PRAY! You don't create the hope; He does. In prayer, is where you put on the armor of God.

The 5 Ps:
Your position of prayer produces power for your promotion.

You can intentionally support your husband by your consistent, positive and pure attitude. Your encouraging prayer support is intentionality with God. As you are led to pray for him, refuse to compare yourself to him, change him, complain about him, or make a list of what he is not doing. His spiritual maturity is up to him and God. Your intentional prayers invite the kind of unity that is required for a thriving relationship.

God is moved by you because you are your husband's helpmate. You help the most when you are a woman of prayer! Over time, the longer you pray like this, the more you will see your husband become the man of your dreams. He will change. He will become a brand new man right in front of your eyes. I've witnessed my very own husband bloom into the very man of God I have always prayed he would be. The prayers of a believing woman changes everything about him. It truly does. So, take heart, lovely, and go read 1 Peter 3.

Remain planted in prayer. Your intentionality about taking every-thing to God will begin to shift your blinding pain. It will diffuse the problems that feel bigger than life, and break down the walls that seem to be closing in around you. God may be ready to give you a miracle, but have you made yourself available? Being your husband's helpmate is praying boldly with faith. You become an advocate for your husband to mature in intimacy with Jesus. His next breath may be the moment you have been believing for, so don't take your eyes off the prize: Jesus' heart. Release what you want to gain from prayer. This is where God will hold all of you as He leads your husband. Get ready to follow into God's greatness.

LISTEN & WATCH

1 Peter 3:1-5,9,11
Wives, be subject to your own husbands, so that even if some do not obey the word, they may be won without a word by the conduct of their wives, when they see your respectful and pure conduct. Do not let your adorning be external - the braiding of hair and the putting on of gold jewelry, or the clothing you wear, but let your adorning be the hidden person of the heart with the imperishable beauty of a gentle and quiet spirit, which in God's sight is very precious. For this is how the holy women who hoped in God used to adorn themselves, by submitting to their own husbands. Do not repay evil for evil or reviling for reviling, but on the contrary, bless, for to this you were called, that you may obtain a blessing. Seek peace and pursue it.

PRAY: *GOD*

Lord, You know all of my failures and fears.

There is nothing you cannot handle.

I bring to You every part of me, even the places I may be

unknowingly hiding behind, so that

You can make something beautiful.

Come and do the same for my beloved husband.

I come before You because I know You are the

Only One who can take all distress and sorrow,

and turn it into glorious hope.

I bring to You a repentant heart, alive and on fire for Jesus

so that I may become radiant from the inside-out.

I don't know how to, but You do. It's what You do.

I am vulnerably and authentically pouring out everything inside

of me: the good, the hopeful, the ugly, & the wrong.

Change me and make me like You. Give me my daily bread.

Show me how to be the wife who refuses to pay evil for evil.

May I be the woman who conducts herself with respect,

modesty, purity, and in all of the femininity and grace you

bestowed upon me. Grant my husband peace as you keep him

from all evil. Bless him in his calling and position as my leader.

Thank you for Your peace and blessing.

JOURNAL PROMPT

How can you intentionally live out 1 Peter 3 today?

DAY 29:
ABIDE IN JESUS

Abiding on the vine is the single most powerful discipline for a thriving, Godly marriage. Jesus must be your Source. Water the well within you with nothing short of God Himself.

Abiding is actively moving towards Jesus, seeking His will, and knocking on doors with open hands instead of closed fists. We come to Jesus with a space for Him to fill. He doesn't always come after us, revealing Himself. This is a two-way relationship. When you go to prayer, seek Him with a surrender that requires all of you. If you come to Jesus with a full glass of yourself, there will not be any room for Him to fill it with His will, and He won't force you. He desires you to want Him.

Prayer and fasting are foundational disciplines for growing in submission to God. Galatians 5:1 reads, "For freedom, Christ has set us free; stand firm therefore, and do not submit again to the yoke of slavery." As you keep in step with the Spirit, you will not gratify the desires of the flesh (Galatians 5:16). This love story of abiding is freedom from flesh! And in Romans 6:20, it asks the question for what fruit are you really getting while being slaves to sin - fruit of lawlessness and impurity. Abiding in God, you will bear much fruit, but apart from Him you can do nothing (John 15:5). So, if we want freedom from division in marriage that comes from self-seeking flesh, wouldn't we readily find out how to abide?

Abiding comes from fellowshipping with God on a level where yielding to Him actually brings you freedom. We do not usually get the outcome of what we think we are praying for, but when we seek, ask, and knock, we receive His bigger and better answers. Abiding is where true transformation occurs: to start looking like the Father. It's where His promises live. It's where His miracles come. Be willing to get pruned, formed, shaped, and cut back. When I was a child, I actually pruned a bush all the way down to a stump. My parents thought I had killed the bush. But that summer, that thing grew back to its original, wild form again. Maybe abiding on the vine is more about allowing the vinedresser to ensure you are bearing fruit than you know. Make your comeback great, sis!

What are you unwilling to give up and lay down to not abide in Him or be in God's will?

We ought to walk in the same way in which He walked. Read 1 John 2:6 and Ephesians 2:10.

Pray in accordance to God's will. Start with the Lord's prayer in Matthew 6:9-15.

THE PRAYER WOMAN

Abides

IN JESUS.

JOHN 15:7

LISTEN & WATCH

John 15:7
If you abide in me, and my words abide in you, ask whatever you wish, and it will be done for you.

1 Corinthians 13:13
Faith, hope, and love abide, these three; but the greatest of these is love.

1 John 4:16
We have come to know and believe the love that God has for us. God is love, and whoever abides in love abides in God, and God abides in him.

Psalm 91:1
He who dwells in the shelter of the Most High will abide in the shadow of the Almighty.

Psalm 25:13
His soul shall abide in well-being, and his offspring shall inherit the land.

PRAY: *ABIDING*

Jesus, You are the author, founder, and perfecter of my faith.

(Hebrews 12:2) In Your Sovereignty, You know all things,

so I pray that You will teach me how to wait upon

You when I cannot see the best answer.

May my husband be blessed more everyday

because of my submission to him and God's mission.

Lord, teach me Your will,

Your ways,

and Your heart.

I pray that You will give my husband eyes to see,

ears to hear, a willing spirit, and open hands

as he seeks Your will and is obedient to

submitting to the cross and to this

God-crafted marriage covenant.

Take the blinders off his heart, that He may run and not walk.

Grant him God's favor, pressed down, shaken, and overflowing.

Abide with him as he abides in You.

Thank you, God, for giving me a husband

who abides in You as a lifestyle,

obedient to the mission,

from glory to glory.

JOURNAL PROMPT

How are you abiding in Jesus today?

DAY 30:
FOR SUCH A TIME AS THIS

Can you tell that I love Esther? I am mentioning her again because her anointing is incredible, and I believe that I live and write with the mantle of it. So my dear lady, my hope is that His anointing oil will drip onto you today.

Esther knew that her purpose was to know her timing, and then walk in grace with it. Have you ever come to your husband with oodles of kindness, but it was the wrong timing for him? What happens? The kind act perhaps goes unseen? Have you ever shown forgiveness or been contrite in an effort to make restitution, but because the timing was premature for him, it just didn't produce resolution? My dear, when he is not ready, take it to the Lord, and release it. Sometimes, being ready to make peace is a good thing because it plants a seed in him to become receptive to where you are, but other times, our efforts can push him farther away. You can write that long text message, or handwritten note that describes your earnest effort for ushering unity back to your marriage as quickly as possible, but if discernment is not used then we can not move the needle at all. In fact, it must be the Spirit of God to do that. Trying too hard to help him see the change or the healing can become a hindrance for him. As a woman, our queen power is in letting go and running to God for wisdom.

Discernment is a major spiritual tool to keep accessible. It is where God guides you in making decisions. He will often place a pause on my thoughts, right in the middle of my decision-making and this reminds me to drop what I am about to do from my own human logic, and in turn, ask Jesus how He wants me to view the circumstance. As your spiritual muscles grow, it becomes easier to drop your finite human understanding and, instead, adopt God's infinite wisdom. He always has a bigger scope because He knows past, present, and future. Using spiritual discernment equips the Prayer Woman to know her timing, her battles, and how to be dressed for each one; dressed in the armor of God and robed with spiritual fruit.

The Prayer Woman knows that she is called for such a time as this, and in her obedience to JESUS' authority over her, she is positioned to:

set the captive free: prays her husband out of it

be a source of strength: doesn't let it get extinguished

stir up revival & unity: admonishes, praises, submits to him

enable peace: doesn't bring the dirty laundry to him

bring joy: she is the joy no matter if he has none

run the race: even in worse conditions, her song gets louder

be faithful: she never stops moving towards him

stand in this covenant: her decisions are under his covering

break the chains of sinful cycles: doesn't respond to them

move the unmovable: never gives up on knowing it'll move

pray that miracle forth: I'm next! This is my promise

This is your mantra today: "Put me in, coach!" Shout it a couple of times so you can hear yourself until you get it deeper into your soul. "Put me in, coach!" God has put you in this position for your husband's good.

LISTEN & WATCH

Matthew 6:6
When you pray, go into your room and shut the door and pray to your Father who is in secret. And your Father who sees in secret will reward you.

Romans 8:26
Likewise, the Spirit helps us in our weakness. For we do not know what to pray for as we ought, but the Spirit, Himself, intercedes for us with groanings too deep for words.

Mark 14:38
Watch and pray that you may not enter into temptation.
The spirit is willing, but the flesh is weak.

Luke 11:2,3
When you pray, say: "Father, hallowed be Your name.
Your kingdom come. Give us each day our daily bread..."

PRAY: *THE TIME IS NOW*

Thank you for knowing exactly where I am, Father.

Today, I know my position is in prayer,

so I come seeking You with everything in me.

I bring You love. I just want to love on You, Abba.

I praise You for calling me Yours.

I praise You for calling my husband Yours.

You have anointed us to be in SUBmission to

Your Mission as You are in COmission with us.

You never leave us, nor forsake us. You appointed the two of us

on this God mission, for such a time as this.

Reveal Your will more clearly everyday.

We are ready and willing. We want to expand the Kingdom

with love, hope, and set the captives free.

Thank you that our marriage is on fire,

that you established us before we ever were born,

and equipped us for ushering Your wonder-working power.

Bind us in more unity than ever before,

so that our influence reaches generations to come.

Thank you for the breakthroughs that You have brought

in me and in my husband during this journey, and for all the

ones that are coming our way.

Thank you for building character and hope.

JOURNAL PROMPT

Write down 3 ways you are in position as a Prayer Woman.

DAY 31:
TURNING PAIN INTO POWER

Have you found yourself fighting the lies with Truth, kicking back the darkness, and living in more Light these past few weeks? I hope so. God's Word and Presence are the only places to take your fight. Wrestle with Him, here, during this fast. Invite Jesus to consume distraction, destroy the lies, and obliterate the temptation to skip spending time with Him.

God's Word and Presence are Your shelter, comfort, plumb line, and defense. Jesus is out in front of you. He kicks down doors, shields you, dispels darkness, and brings peace. He has not missed a single moment of pain or drop of tears that you have shed. When you ache, He knows. He feels the pain from your sin and the sin done to you. And He alone can use this pain to turn it into power and glory.

The Prayer Woman believes that her victory, from pain to power, from tears to triumph, and from ash to beauty is held in Jesus. She might not see the victory at this time. It may still be held up in the Heavens. She may even have completely given up on it because the heartache of desire is too much to bear. If you are anything like me, you understand a lot about the place where hope is lost, where the heart becomes numb because too many wrong things have happened; the place where there is no way it can turn around; the forgotten miracle, where the dream skipped over you; your prayers didn't work. Here is the turning point: *It is only by Love and through Love that you were made, lovely woman.*

Love is the reason for how you live, because Jesus is Love, and He is within you. But there is a battle against love. This very real and ugly battle comes to threaten our hope, discourage our courage, blur our vision, tempt, steal, and cause chaos to the unity God founded for your marriage.

But Jesus - Love is His name - came to cover a multitude of sins and cast out fear and bind wounds. Do you see that Love has the power to create something out of nothing? So, go ahead and don't be afraid of your tears and pain, because God will come in the middle of it and CREATE a beauty from your ashes. Love creates new life where there may be death. Love transforms. Love renews. Love heals. Love sets free. Love is the single source of our identity as daughters of the King. So, Love is our pulse in marriage. Love is our compass and catalyst for more love. Love is the multiplier: if all you have is a mustard seed size, it's enough for God. And if you don't, He will create it and rescue you. The devil schemes to divide you and your husband: your favor, unity, love, position, & calling in Jesus. Everything you are centered in is Love, so satan wars constantly against the center of you. When this fierce battle rages against your story of love: loving God, loving yourself, wanting to be loved, to give love, and for someone to receive your love, you must AWAKEN! Open your spiritual eyes to resist feeding a deficit. Resist adopting pain. Do not let it enter your being. Here is where tears stream down our faces in buckets, where our knees hit the ground, where we feel like we cannot hope. If all you can see is the pain, rest in knowing that Love creates a way; and the power to get up and walk in victory is available right now.

You are Loved, So Stand in Love.

LISTEN & WATCH

Psalm 116:8,9
For you have delivered my soul from death, my eyes from tears, my feet from stumbling; I will walk before the Lord in the land of the living.

Psalm 126:6
He who goes out weeping, bearing the seed for sowing, shall come home with shouts of joy, bringing his sheaves with him.

2 Corinthians 5:17
Therefore, if anyone is in Christ, he is a new creation. The old has passed away; behold, the new has come.

1 John 3:9
No one born of God makes a practice of sinning, for God's seed abides in him; and he cannot keep on sinning because he has been born of God.

PRAY: *GOD TURNS PAIN INTO POWER BY LOVE*

Father, You see my pain and You see my victory.

You are the Victor of my head and of my marriage.

The thief will not steal by day or by night

what is my Heavenly birthright.

I cast off every ounce of brokenness,

and shed what I must unbecome in order to have more of You!

Bottle my tears and turn them into glory.

I relinquish what I think I must have and what little I know.

Take the wheel and be all that You are: Bigger!

Comfort every part of my husband's heart. Hold every single tear

and point of pain; from the time he was born to this very second.

Take him Back To The Garden, where he can start over in You.

Guide him in the shedding of his scars.

Give him feeling where he has become numb.

Give him a clean slate, washed by the blood of the Lamb,

purified, sanctified, redeemed, yes, but even more than this,

take him to the well of Living Water.

May he be Found In The River of healing and transformation.

Wash him in Love.

Turn every single teardrop that has and has not been able to roll

down my husband's face, into a reason for triumph because You

were there in the middle of the worst. You have turned the mess

into his success and those battle wounds into power.

JOURNAL PROMPT

What tears and point of pain are you giving God today?

DAY 32:
THE JOYFUL SURRENDER

Sometimes we fall short from finding that joyful place in the surrender. It happens when we idolize the lie that 'we already tried and it should be enough'. That idol is rooted in self-image; the old man in us, refusing to surrender it all. Self wants to give only in part and hold on to the rest. It took me a long time to give God the stone in my heart where this idol was keeping me small, and definitely lacking in His joy. Becoming undone hurts our pride. Yeah, it hurt mine, until the Holy Spirit kept nudging me to repentance. I couldn't surrender to Him all of my hopes, dreams, plans, or control of my life before because I wanted to ensure I got what I wanted. But all of that was a lie. When I held on, I actually lost. And that's playing god. It robbed a lot from my life for many years. God's Word teaches us to humble ourselves (1 Peter 5:6), and deny ourselves as we daily pick up the cross and follow Him. So, the joy you may think you will find by ensuring life goes a certain way, is plainly not surrender to God. As I am crucified with Christ, it is no longer I who live, but Christ who lives within me (Galatians 2:20). In God's Word it says, "If you keep my commandments, you will abide in my love, just as I have kept my Father's commandments and abide in His love. These things I have spoken to you, that my joy may be in you, and that your joy may be full."

Are you ready for joy to be made full in your marriage? Joy is much greater than being happy. His joy is made full by abiding in Him, laying down your life, and following the one Way (John 14:6).

Do you want your life to be good enough or great?

Will you commit today to going beyond what selfishness wants, in only giving a little and reaching its limits?

Do you want your marriage to be for the two of you, or to reach beyond those walls for a Kingdom impact?

The shift is part of your original design, from back in the Garden of Eden. It is already inside of you. It lives, but it needs to be awakened and set free. You are about to be set on fire. Keep chasing God and you will begin to thrive and flourish; not in earthly terms, but for eternity. Set eternity upon your heart, and watch a power rise in your marriage that you long for but maybe don't know about it yet. Your power as a Godly wife is in your joyful surrender of self: it's the opposite of what the world teaches, for sure.

It's not about achieving success, things of this world, or earthly statuses. **The point of surrender is purity**: to be stripped down, peeled back layer after layer to find what God intended for you from the beginning. Without surrender, we cannot come to complete purity. Without purity, we do not have much power. Without the active power of God in our lives, how do we minister love? Love is the essence of healing. It creates and restores.

Do you want to surrender all yet? Proverbs 17:22 says, "a joyful heart is good medicine, but a crushed spirit dries up the bones." Behold, let the shofar sound as you break forth into a joyous new song, for He is our Rock. Your soul will be satisfied as with fat and rich food, and your mouth will praise you with joyful lips" Psalm 63:5. There is truly nothing better than being in courts of praise.

LISTEN & WATCH

1 Peter 5:6
Humble yourselves, therefore, under the mighty hand of God so that at the proper time he may exalt you.
James 4:7
Submit yourselves therefore to God. Resist the devil, and he will flee from you.
Luke 9:23
And he said to all, "If anyone would come after me, let him deny himself and take up his cross daily and follow me."
Colossians 3:18
Wives, submit to your husbands, as is fitting in the Lord.
Proverbs 17:22
A joyful heart is good medicine, but a crushed spirit dries up the bones.
Psalm 95:1
Oh come, let us sing to the Lord; let us make a joyful noise to the rock of our salvation!
Psalm 98:6
With trumpets and the sound of the horn make a joyful noise before the King, the Lord!

PRAY: *SURRENDER*

Lord, I surrender what I want, when I want it, how I want, and all of

the above. Forgive me for putting my needs and desires above my

husband's. While the world is crazed with making sure

women are heard, I am a woman whose identity is in Jesus.

Jesus, you are the only confidence I need and in You I am

completely known. All of my needs are met in Jesus:

intimacy, safety, protection, compassion, everything!

When I think I am lacking, bring me to repentance.

I am a steward of your Goodness

in the covenant God crafted and gave me.

I didn't design or form this marriage, so I won't start adding in

ingredients of my own desire. God, You know what it takes.

I am here, joyfully surrendering what it looks like.

Move for my husband's good. Remind him of how

You gave the perfect example of surrender.

We devote this marriage to be all about You and not about us.

Bless my husband with integrity, purity, and holiness.

Grant him more joy than he has ever known possible.

May he burst with exceeding and abundant, inner joy!

Because of his Godly surrender,

increase the strength of his spirit.

Come, waves of a new song in his soul.

DAY 32

JOURNAL PROMPT

What do you need to surrender that may bring spiritual fruit to your husband?

DAY 33:
YOUR TRUMP CARD

Here it is, your trump card: Inward Beauty. Inward beauty trumps and triumphs over fading outward beauty. The Prayer Woman is the sister who exhorts her fellow sister in Christ. Her countenance is the lamp of her soul, the spirit within her, and the mantle of authority and power she carries because Christ is her King. We have all been around the kind of women who try to make victims of other women, pushing them down rather than esteeming them in their real identity. That's not you.

You, woman, are a lady who knows her identity in Christ, so she knows that her sisters are also known and divinely called. This tribe of sisterhood bands together because Jesus is the center. With Jesus as the center, the Prayer Woman does not compare herself to other sisters, because she is rooted in her true identity. She does not elevate herself at the expense of a sister. She does not gossip about or smear a sister's name or tell her that her looks are not good enough or that her bad choices will follow her again.

My dear, the world will always be out to trip you up, knock you down, and blind you. But the attacks are weak and false. The attacks are lies, with the devil behind the scheme. Your powerful, inner beauty comes from the God who lives within you and the aura you set around you. God doesn't pick the special, the rich, the most beautiful, the lucky; no, He doesn't have favorites. Will you answer your calling to walk radiantly redeemed?

The spirit of a wise woman is radiant and pure. She is known by the fruit of her labor. When you read Proverbs 31, there is not one single verse that talks about her looks. What does it say? An excellent wife is far more precious than jewels. She dresses herself in strength, she is giving, prepared, has a routine, is disciplined, resourceful, skillful, generous, and she is not idle. She does not copy the rest of the world, but lives set apart, holy and acceptable in God's sight.

This is your Trump Card! You swim against the tide. You do not comply with the norm. You are uniquely made by God. You are heir to the Kingdom of Heaven. You believe bigger. Proverbs 31:30 says, "Charm is deceitful, and beauty is vain, but a woman who fears the Lord is to be praised." The fear of the Lord is the beginning of wisdom. You are this woman. The Prayer Woman is the Proverbs 31 woman.

You know that you were wonderfully made by God, and are perfected in Christ. Pair that with your devotion to putting Jesus first in all you do and say, and that's your plumb line. Everything shy of it are toy arrows that bounce off of you without notice because you are protected and preoccupied with being a Warrior Queen! Let me hear you ROAR, sister! Your queendom is your inner beauty; safe and secure in Jesus. There is not a thing nor a person that can diminish or steal it from you. It's yours! It was custom crafted, uniquely and intricately designed; freely given by the King of Love. You were fashioned perfectly with a purpose to flourish in agape love. Your power as a wife is being the radiant bride who keeps her eyes focused on Jesus, not by the noise of the world. Glow from the inside out. Get up and go attract your husband with your trump card.

LISTEN & WATCH

1 Peter 3:4
Let your adorning be the hidden person of the heart with the imperishable beauty of a gentle and quiet spirit, which in God's sight is very precious.

Psalm 139:14
I praise You, for I am fearfully and wonderfully made. Wonderful are Your works; my soul knows it very well.

1 Peter 2:9
But you are a chosen generation, a royal priesthood, a holy nation, a people for His own possession, that you may proclaim the excellencies of Him who called you out of darkness into His marvelous light.

Ephesians 2:10
For we are His workmanship, created in Christ Jesus for good works, which God prepared beforehand, that we should walk in them.

1 Corinthians 3:16
Do you not know that you are God's temple and that God's Spirit dwells in you?

PRAY: *HELP ME KNOW HIS HEART*

By God's restoring power living in us, help my husband and I to trust You and be vulnerable with each other, even after every time we get hurt. May we find healing in You quickly so that we can get back to doing the work of the Kingdom, rather than feeding selfishness. Father, give me insight on all the ways my husband serves me. Open my eyes when I become numb or blind. Develop and deepen my appreciation for how he loves me. Make me a trustworthy wife. Show me the position of his heart, God, and how I can deliver my words with tenderness, in the ways that best support him. Seal our trust as far as the east is from the west, with no more digging up the old.
The old me is cancelled. The new me is restored.
Show him where he is safe to stand; that I support him, cheer for him, stand with him, and hold him up. Keep him close to You, Lord, so that He walks in his husband role that You created for him. Keep him running to You, close to Your heart, One with You so that he can be one with me: in spirit, mind, body, and mission. Spirit of God, rest upon my husband so that everyday he knows who he is in You better than the day before. You are a Great God and You have an amazing calling on his life to bring You glory. Complete the great work you began in him and set his soul on fire for Jesus, more everyday.

JOURNAL PROMPT

Ask the Lord to give you eyes to see your husband's love for you: open heart, open eyes, open fist.

DAY 34:
JOY

Joy is for the taking this day! It is fruit from Holy Spirit, and it is all yours, my dear. My prayer over you is that when joy feels like the last thing available in you or around you, that this will be the very thing that begins to bubble up just from reading this blessing.

You might be thinking: that sounds nice, but I'm in so deep over here, all I feel like is crumbling in tears, taking a nap, or throwing up a peace out sign. First of all, if you need to cry or take a nap, do it. Your strength becomes renewed when you take care of yourself and give yourself permission to relax, rest, have a good cry, journal, go on a walk, or take a nap. Sometimes, I'll even just sit on the porch and stare at leaves blowing in the wind to empty my head, or close my eyes and listen to the birds sing. But if you want to quit: dig deeper. There is a well of faith. Don't give up. You will find joy more quickly when you release any blockages of lies or busyness.

JOY - where does it come from and why do you need it for unity in your marriage? Wife, when the Lord's joy grows within you because of your time spent with Him, it activates other necessary tools like grace, meekness, boldness, and courage. You will begin to notice how joy sets you free from fear, and from playing small with blessing your husband. Without joy, you can feel intimidated, overcome, weak, and tired. You become limited and develop a noticeable bandwidth of pressures and responsibilities. God's joy ignites an energy within your soul to grow more of its fruit. Joy is like a magnet; it attracts love, comfort, compassion, and intimacy. James 1:2 says that even when we are facing nothing but difficulties, look at it as an invaluable opportunity to experiences the greatest joy that you can. No, joy isn't happiness. It's not something you make or get through having it easy. It's produced by endurance, in becoming perfected by the Father, in full reliance upon His Spirit, until there is nothing missing and nothing lacking. That is your promise, written in the Word of God. Read James.

Joy is not always going to take the form of a bubbly, fun-loving, lighthearted, and playful interaction, but you will know you have it because the joy of the Lord is a strength that endures every trial. When you practice putting on the breastplate of faith and love (1 Thessalonians 5:8), you will count it all joy even when you are tested. Even in marriage disagreements and pain, where that charisma hides, what do you have left? If you allow your energy to become robbed that easily, then you probably either didn't have the Lord's joy in you, or you chose to give it away for free. Girl, go get it and hold on to it like it is the gold it is. The joy of the Lord is your strength and your song. (Psalm 118:14)

God is in control - this is your confident joy! This is your steadfast resolve that everything is going to be alright. Praise your way through it, to it, and don't stop there. Joy is not about feeling happy. Marriage is not about your happiness either; it's about living as an holy fragrance as an offering of glory to God. In joy, you have an overflow from Jesus, that is not dependent upon earthly circumstances. The Prayer Woman can laugh with strength because this is her original design. God is within her, and He is joy! When everything else is sinking sand, she stands upon the solid rock of JOY! He is her salvation.

LISTEN & WATCH

Galatians 5:22
The fruit of the spirit is...Joy!
John 15:10,11
Abide in my love...that My joy may be in you, that your joy may be full.
Hebrews 12:2
Looking to Jesus, the founder and perfecter of our faith, who for the joy that was set before him endured the cross, despising the shame, and is seated at the right hand of the throne of God.
Romans 12:12
Rejoice in hope, be patient in tribulation, be constant in prayer.
John 16:24
...Ask and you will receive, that your joy may be full.

PRAY: *REJOICE AND TAKE JOY*

Joy is mine!

Fill me with this real fruit, Lord, so that it lasts and endures

the tests of time and the refining in marriage.

I take joy as my strength this day, and delight in knowing that

when my playful and charismatic moods don't last,

YOU always last in me.

Lord, I pray deliverance over my husband right now.

Touch his mind, soul, body, emotions, and spirit,

Lord, with the powerful fruit of JOY!

Bubble up within him a childlike giddyness,

uncontrollable laughter and glee.

Fill him with Your Goodness!

May his lungs expand and his voice echo throughout the

house as he belts out a new song! Yes, Lord, I love repeating this

one in prayer because its Your beauty that moves me

and calls me to believe for the worshipper to arise.

Rejoice over him and he rejoices in you.

Don't let it be for a moment, but let this true joy

be everlasting and have fortitude

through every storm.

Let a jubilee arise in my household this day!

JOURNAL PROMPT

Write down three areas you can REJOICE over today.

DAY 35:
GRACE

In your quest for a Biblical, fruitful life, grace and mercy come running. You already know that you will continue to become unrecognizable in the new growth as you spend more time in God's presence. But failure is part of the journey. It makes us humble and proves our need for Him. There are both mountains and valleys. What kind of woman you are in both places might vary as you are maturing. Ask God to give you His strength to be able to rejoice in your suffering. It will produce endurance, which produces character, and character produces hope, and hope does not put us to shame, because God's love has been poured into our hearts through the Holy Spirit, who has been given to us. (Romans 5:3-5)

You are in a process of perfection in Christ, the continual reliance upon Him as your hope, as you receive His free gift: grace. Nothing you could ever do, or earn, or become would grant you this gift. Grace lives outside of you, but it is for you. Through faith you have been saved, and from God's sacrifice, you have this new gift of starting over. Forgiven, transformed, and redeemed. His grace is more than enough to cover your sin and wash you clean as snow. Sin will not conquer you, for God already has (Romans 6:14). You weren't made to get it perfect all the time. You were made for needing a Savior. That is why marriage is a three-corded strand; for Jesus to be Sufficient when we clearly come up short.

When growth seems slow, when growth gets covered up by rehashed sin, when God needs to prune us once more...your Master Gardener always tends with grace. He came to yield His harvest of glory, yes, but He is gentle and kind. He knows our limits, and He knows just what to give us for the call beyond them. Grace is God's free gift we do not deserve, but given so that we can thrive and flourish in the Garden of marriage. Stand in grace when you become weak. Let go of perfection. Yes, we are fallible creatures. We will fail. We will sin. We will not always be able to peddle forward, keep the momentum, and not rock the boat. Sometimes we do get a little lost in ourselves and forget that God has what we need. Repent.

This is your gentle reminder that while you are doing your best, remember to breathe. Remember that you are free to fail. You are a work in progress. God is weeding, cultivating, tending, pruning, and watering you. In a similar way, your faithfulness and obedience is being tended to daily, and in doing so it gets hard.

God knows this; that is why His grace covers and provides when we feel the burnout, the burdens, and the pressures. Cry out for more of Jesus! The more you seek to know Christ, the more you will be changed into His likeness. It does not happen overnight. This is a journey of refining and sanctification. Draw near to Him as He draws near to you (James 4:8). Be cleansed. Be purified in your heart, and do not be double-minded. God's power will be made perfect in your weakness. Do not fear your weaknesses. Boast of them so that Christ may rest upon you. When you misstep, get back on track by getting in His presence to repent, turn, and obey. Forgive others as He forgives you. Forgive your husband for holding anything against you, if he did. As you are connected to the source of grace, you can now give him back the same grace you receive from the Father. He has more than enough.

LISTEN & WATCH

2 Corinthians 12:9
He said to me, "My grace is sufficient for you, for my power is
made perfect in weakness." Therefore, I will boast all the more
gladly of my weaknesses, so that the power of Christ may rest
upon me.

Ephesians 2:8,9
For by grace you have been saved through faith. And this is not
your own doing; it is the gift of God, not a result of works, so that
no one may boast.

Hebrews 4:16
Let us then with confidence draw near to the throne of grace, that
we may receive mercy and find grace in time of need.

Romans 6:14
For sin will have no dominion over you, since you are not under
law but under grace.

Psalm 51:9
Hide your face from my sins, and blot out all my inquities.

Romans 11:6
But if it is by God's grace, it is no longer on the basis of works;
otherwise grace would no longer be grace.

PRAY: *MADE PERFECT IN WEAKNESS*

Abba, thank you that Your power is made perfect in my

weaknesses; that You are always enough.

Thank you for forgiving me every time I fail.

Thank you for forgiving my husband every time he fails.

We are held in your grace and mercy,

and for this I am overjoyed that sin has no hold on us.

We are free to fail. Only alive in You.

I praise You for both the victories and the downfalls

because I see now that You have never loosed Your grip on us.

There is nothing I can ever do to lose Your love.

May grace and mercy flow faithfully within my husband.

Pour Your grace through me so I am void of

judgment and discouragement.

As my husband walks in Your grace,

I thank You for renewed strength in the shadow of Your wings.

I praise You for every wound, old behavior and mindset

that is being cut off right now because of Your dominion.

Unworthiness, stony heart, all pain be

found and healed in the river of God. All trauma healed.

Go God! You are Great!

JOURNAL PROMPT

How can you accept God's grace today for yourself,
then give grace to your husband?

DAY 36:
THE KING'S TABLE

You are invited to sit at the King's Table. Come feast upon the grandeur, feast upon the richest treasures on earth. The Lord's supper has been served for your marriage. There is the meat of endurance, the fruit of patience, the cup of joy, the seat of mercy, the medicine of laughter. It's all here! There is more than enough for all of you. God has prepared this exact table, with your name on it, the name by which He calls you. It has your husband's name on it, and it has a third name etched into the wooden planks of the assigned seat as well: JESUS!

Prayer Woman, as a Godly wife, you have already taken a seat at this table where you, your husband, and Jesus sit together as the three-corded strand. (Ecclesiastes 4:12) You are uneasily broken, but you have free will. Jesus provided this table before you came into His covenant, and before He gave you His covenant of marriage with your husband. He sits here now, and He will be sitting here until you meet Him up in the clouds. All that you will ever need to thrive in your marriage, is on this table. But if you decide to stand up and walk away from it, it's your choice.

To stay seated, is to stay in God's Joy and Peace. It is to feast upon the available Heavenly resources. In marriage, as you know, there will be times, where one of you decides to not drink or eat, shove away the plate, or even to stand and turn from the table.

I have been in both places: both seated and standing. I have been on both sides of the coin as well, holding on to the hand of a spouse who will not sit or eat with me at the King's table, and the other way around. Where are you? The victim mindset that is rooted in pride comes from a person who is not seated. The "I can never get it right", "I'm always wrong", "I cannot seem to make you happy"....you know the words you say or hear. Make your list, then lay it down in front of you and pray the prayer on the next page, because this is where you take your seat.

If you seek peace: **sit.**
If you seek to know how to love your husband: **sit.**
If you seek to know his heart: **sit.**
If your well is empty: **sit.**
If you are bringing your lack to your husband: **sit.**
If you are controlling: **sit.**
If all you can see are the problems: **sit.**

Woman, your self-leadership in your prayer life will absolutely draw him to pivot on his heels back to the table to take a seat and gorge upon the feast of the Lord. But it is not in your doing; it's in the timing and will of God. This is God's feast, not yours. If you serve up your goods to convince him to eat or to stay or to love you, you will run out, run short, run dry, and never satisfy.

To be seated at the King's Table is to abide on the vine! Abiding in Jesus is the key. He is the well of living water which satisfies and pours out more than enough. He will water your well because He is the Source of all you need.

When Jesus is your source, you no longer have the need to change your husband or prove yourself to him or anyone else. Instead, now you rest, being still in God, as you pray for God's will.

LISTEN & WATCH

Ecclesiastes 4:12
And though a man might prevail against one who is alone, two will withstand him - a threefold cord is not quickly broken.
Psalm 23:1-3
The Lord is my Shepherd; I shall not want. He makes me lay down in green pastures. He leads me beside still waters. He restores my soul. He leads me in paths of righteousness for His name's sake.
1 Corinthians 10:21
You cannot drink the cup of the Lord and the cup of demons.
You cannot partake of table of the Lord and the table of demons.
John 15:4
Abide in me, and I in you. As the branch cannot bear fruit by itself, unless it abides in the vine, neither can you, unless you abide in me.
Matthew 5:44
Love your enemies and pray for those who persecute you, so that you may be sons of your Father who is in heaven.

PRAY: *SEATED*

Great Shepherd, Master Teacher,

teach me what it means to sit at the King's Table.

I said 'yes' to sitting here, as wife, when I got married,

so, Father, instruct me and my husband to know how to eat

from this prepared place and nowhere else.

Shelter us from looking at other tables.

Keep our blinder's on, to see only what You have for us,

as You faithfully keep the invitation open for us to

stay seated. Bind the enemy from deceiving us,

and gird up our spirit to know the difference.

I sit here because I cannot live without Your peace.

There is nothing but death in turning to leave this table.

So, I cling to my husband's hand, to sit together,

and feed him Life, the food of respect, honor, agape love,

and peace. I refuse to allow the food from another table,

or the food of the enemy to enter my being. It is but dung.

And when it is thrown at me, I choose to still sit.

Lord, I give you my husband completely. He is not mine, but Yours.

I am but a steward of Your covenant, and a sister to Him

in Christ. Thank you for placing us at our marriage table with You.

Everything we need to sow into each other is here.

JOURNAL PROMPT

How are you sitting down? Are you thriving in the fruit of meekness, humility, patience, joy, respect, and honor?

DAY 37:
MESS TO SUCCESS

God is not surprised by your mess. Whether it's a messy moment or a messy life, you do not shock Him. Abba longs for us to empty out all of the emotions that we become too full of, that bubble up within us like a raging river. It must bubble up and out: unaddressed compromise, anger, unmet needs, confusion, and frustration. What tips your boat?

What happens when you stuff down your ungodly reactions for too long without dealing with them? They begin to build pressure in your heart and mind until it becomes too much to keep at bay. All the while, you are trying to operate in the fruit of the Spirit to your husband, but this involuntary reaction must come out. Sometimes it is vomited all over him, without grace, without God's Spirit. It just comes out in full form of ugliness and ends up causing disaster, division, and pain. Maybe we thought the right thing was to suppress and minimize it in order to increase our Biblical response. But there is a way to let go and let God have it all.

Here's the raw truth, we were born into sin. We have the old man (Ephesians 4, Colossians 3:9) biting back every chance he can get, and then there's the devil who preys upon our mess, but here is the Good News: God doesn't love you any less or is surprised by your sin. Your weakness just shows your need of Him, and that is beautiful! Your discipline, as a Prayer Woman, becomes refined by getting closer to the fire, to holiness; the place where His presence lives. Come as you are to Jesus! His holy presence is what builds your spirit and develops your habits. If something happens in your marriage that makes you want to react in a way you know is not pure, and all you can do is hide and kick under your bed sheets, or scream into your pillow; do it! The Bible says in Psalm 4:4, "Be angry, and do not sin; ponder in your own hearts on your beds, and then be silent." Sometimes, before getting silent, the devil has got to flee. The flesh has to know that its vacancy is up. So repent to get it up and out, give it to Jesus, and then find the silence that comes over you. It will.

This is the job of the Holy Spirit: to reach into the depths of your soul, to the root, under all of our broken layers, and pull out the mess within you, so that the Father is unveiled. He wants to smooth every path and wash with His cleansing power, every single crevice, wrinkle, & blemish so that, today, you walk in your purpose as His pure bride.

You become pure in Jesus first, so that you can live as a pure bride on earth to your husband. Take a look in the mirrow at yourself instead of pointing the finger of blame. Purity comes through Jesus and the blood of His Lamb. When you run to your prayer closet to take your mess; take it all and then don't leave that place. Don't get up from your knees or leave your room UNTIL Jesus is holding it all and you feel His oil upon your head. You will know by His peace that surpasses your understanding. You will know when you walk into the next room and your husband or child says something that could disrupt your spirit, you stand there in a calm, patient, poised and collected stance, and it rolls right off your shoulder. Now go to your husband and bless him with the shining countenance of Jesus.

LISTEN & WATCH

1 Corinthians 11:3
The head of every man is Christ, the head of the wife is her husband, and the head of Christ is God.

Ephesians 5:23
For the husband is the head of the wife even as Christ is the head of the church, his body, and it himself its Savior.

Philippians 3:14
I press on toward the goal for the prize of the upward call of God in Christ Jesus.

1 John 1:9
If we confess our sins, He is faithful and just to forgive us and to cleanse us from all unrighteousness.

PRAY: *THE MESS IS GOD'S*

God, I'm messy. I'm unrefined. I have issues and things I want to

go a certain way. I have desires to be fulfilled. I have old beliefs

about how I want to live, be treated, and be married,

but they are all dead now.

I am here to be remade on the Vine & serve this present mission.

I can not and will not do this covenant marriage without You.

I invite you to take all of me, empty me of ME so that my

capacity for You is increased to overflowing.

Expand my borders. Restore what has been lost.

Thank you for showing me that I no longer have to live perfectly,

that in my mistakes, Your blood covers me. You produce the fruit.

I'm here abiding in You. Do what You came to do, God!

Prune, uproot, transplant, whatever You want in Your garden.

Lord, this marriage is Yours. I am not the Head, you are.

I do not pretend to know the steps to more unity in my

marriage. Praise you, Good Father, for being the Head of my

husband, that his heart safely trusts in you. As he takes his

mess to You, make way for peace to overwhelm him. When he

hits a wall or cycle that isn't of You, cancel its lying power that

keeps him cycling. When he doesn't know how to believe he is

worthy, I call forth the One who is over all:

His name is Jesus!

JOURNAL PROMPT

What mess are you giving to God right now?

DAY 38:
GOD HEARS THE WIFE

Lovely woman, your life is laid down, and the strength you now live by is not your own but from Christ living in you. Do you realize that you are royalty? You are God's own precious daughter, with access to His riches of love and mercy. There is no obstacle too big that He cannot cover. There is no detail too tiny that He skips over.

When you pray, God hears you, wife.

You do not need to book an appointment with God. He is already, always present, waiting on you. He wants to fellowship with you, His friend, more often than you know. If you can allow this picture to sink into your heart, you would know that whatever you ask according to His will, it is Yes and Amen.

Sometimes, you won't yet see the fruition of the yes and amen. God's harvest looks much bigger than hope. Trust in Him. His love never fails. He cannot forget about you. If you feel like He forgot about you, or that He is not answering your prayers, or you cannot hear His voice anymore; fear not. Ask Jesus to show you *His will*. He will give you the courage to release your will so that you can see His. Become emptied out.

There is nothing more you can do, nothing better or more right, that will earn God's attentive ear. He always listens and knows your heart (Psalm 139). Rest in this promise! When you pray, your prayers move the heart of God. He is moved with compassion. Pray God-sized, bold prayers! If you can already imagine your petition coming true, then you are not putting faith into it. When you pray for the seemingly impossible and inconceivable, God will ask of you, in return, more than you think you have to offer. But as you obey, He always provides...because He hears you, wife.

As you press further in to your prayer life, you will discover the intimate relationship God has with the praying wife. She is kind, wise, hardworking, creative and strong. She is honoring, respectful, and virtuous. She is loyal, courageous, fearless, dignified, prepared, and energetic. These are traits given to you from God! I don't know about you, but this sounds like the kind of friend I would like to have. She sounds amazing!

Take hold of courage, woman. When you face overwhelming trials, difficult and unexpected situations, when fear knocks on your door, who hears you? God does! When you think you are about to drown, who saves you? Will you forget that God hears your prayers and is able and ready to help you keep your eyes on Him? Lift up a mighty voice and pray. There is no fear in love. Jesus has already conquered the grave. He is Your defender. We need only to call upon His name. Take authority over the fears and the lies by letting Him hear you cry out. Stand in the power of the living Word of God. Use the Scriptures on the next page to pray aloud in your quiet time today.

As your husband's helper, your prayers before the Lord maximize the powerful impact you have on your husband.

Never underestimate the power of prayer for aligning your marriage to God's will, miracles, favor, and blessing.

LISTEN & WATCH

Mark 11:24
Therefore, I tell you, whatever you ask in prayer, believe that you have received it, and it will be yours.

Romans 10:9
If you confess with your mouth that Jesus is Lord and believe in your heart that God raised him from the dead, you will be saved.

James 1:6
But let him ask in faith, with no doubting, for the one who doubts is like a wave in the sea that is driven and tossed by the wind.

John 14:1
Let not your hearts be troubled. Believe in God; believe also in me.

2 Timothy 3:16,17
All Scripture is breathed out by God and profitable for teaching, for reproof, for correction, and for training in righteousness.

Romans 10:17
Faith comes by hearing, and hearing by the word of God.

Hebrews 1:1
Now faith is the assurance of things hoped for, the conviction of things not seen.

PRAY: *PRAY BIGGER*

Lord, I know that You hear me,

so I am praying bigger today than I ever have before.

My faith is expanding for miracles!

By faith, I receive greater grace and reap a harvest

of bountiful victory in You.

I am blessed with favor so these locked doors

must open, provision is here and

these walls must crumble.

My husband is so blessed with divine favor that his

enemies are at peace, favor is increased, and he has powerful

influence for the Kingdom of God. All that my husband places his

hands upon brings glory to Father, and Your favor follows him.

Bless my husband beyond measure with wisdom, discernment,

integrity, purity, leadership, submission to You, and great Love.

Take his sorrow and fill him with joy.

Mend the broken paths. Make straight the ones ahead.

Birth in him the desire for more of You.

Remove pain, sickness, and death from him.

Break the bondage of sin and keep him secure in chastity,

with a single eye, removing every distraction from him.

Keep eternity in his heart.

JOURNAL PROMPT

Write down a few ways you know God has heard you during this 41-day prayer and fasting journey.

DAY 39:
DOING HIM GOOD

When it comes to doing your husband good, and not harm (Proverbs 31:12), what is the first thing that comes to mind? Is it excitement with a smile? Or is it fear? Remember, that as a Prayer Woman, you are interceding on behalf of your husband *for* his good, whether he has been good or harmful to you.

As a woman who fears the Lord, your honor is always unto the Lord. If you are in a hard place, an unsafe place, wrecked emotionally, wherever you are, Jesus knows. He knows exactly what you need so that your prayers illuminate your spirit right out of any pit. When you pray for his good, pray with a yielded spirit. Separate your faith-filled prayers from the fears telling you that can't respect him because of how he is acting right now. God can shift any person, any circumstance, and heal any pain. Do you believe that? Your husband's identity is not in his actions or in his behavior. He is God's son.

If you are not the woman you long to be, or know God needs you to be in your circumstance, RISE up! If your husband is not acting within the Holy Spirit or in his Godly role: PRAY! Get on your knees, beloved. Doing your husband good instead of harm, is to view him through Jesus' eyes: remade, rewritten, whole, healed, delivered, and set free. You will only get this perspective by spending time abiding on the vine: in His Word & in His Presence. You can try to do good in your own power, from your own perspective, from a woman's vantage point, but come up short every time. You will miss the boat completely if we do not ask our husband what he needs from his wife as well as from the Father. Most likely, responses may be something like: be more sensitive to his world, that his tone with you might not be because of you but from something he is dealing with outside the home. Perhaps your husband will tell you that doing him good is just spending time with him, quietly being in each other's presence, instead of bringing him long conversation with anticipations or expectations. It's accepting who he is at the core, without wishing he were different, trying to change him, or lacking something in your identity because of him.

Doing him good is having a peaceful spirit in your tone and words; ensuring that grace and honey are on your tongue. Doing him good is speaking well of him outside the home around others. Exhorting and praising him in front of people stirs up the Spirit of God in your marriage. I have witnessed countless times where my husband calls or texts me a love note immediately after I have just said something praiseworthy in my mind, heart, word, or deed, without him even knowing it. This happens because Jesus formed marriage as a spiritual union. What you do, say, think, and how you live in the hours spent apart from each other absolutely affects the environment for when you come back together.

The Prayer Woman is loyal, willing, open & compassionate. She is actively guarding her mind about him. She positions her husband in her heart for believing his best! Even when she has no proof that he is behaving in his highest version of himself, she believes it, exhorts him in it, and praises him in it. She lives at his side at all times.

LISTEN & WATCH

Psalm 115:11
You who fear the Lord, trust in the Lord! He is their help and their shield.

Psalm 118:4
Let those who fear the Lord say, "His steadfast love endures forever."

Ephesians 5:33
...Let the wife see that she respects her husband.

Ephesians 5:24
Now as the church submits to Christ, so also wives should submit in everything to their husbands.

Zechariah 4:6
Not by might, nor by power, but by my Spirit, says the Lord.

Luke 21:19
By your endurance you will gain your lives.

PRAY: *GOOD AND NOT HARM*

Father, give me Your perspective for how You see my husband,

that this would be the only way I see and treat him.

May it bless my soul, inspire my heart, clear my mind, and grow a

fortitude in my spirit that only You can grow in me.

This is where I stand: in You, for him.

Bind every temptation to test him or set him up.

Purge every form of evil, selfish pride, ego, and idolatry.

It's not my role to show him where to grow.

Everyday, show me how to be a better helpmate.

Guard my mind when I am weak. Move me away from thoughts

that try to trap me and keep me from believing in my husband's

good. Put a hedge of protection over my mind as I stand guard to

prohibit false influences, doubt, and fear. Wrap me in peace so that

my prayers are praise, exhortation, love, and goodwill towards him.

You are trustworthy, Jesus.

Give me the courage to bless him when I don't know how.

Get me unstuck, and into abiding in Your Spirit.

Now, Father, I bless my husband with honor, respect, and peace.

I help him stand when he is weak. I believe the best in him.

I am full of empathy, compassion, comfort, and a listening heart.

My husband is to be praised for he is good.

JOURNAL PROMPT

What are 3 ways you can do him good today?

1) Bring Peace, 2) Praise him 3) Show him you believe in his best.

DAY 40:
KNOWN IN THE GATES

"Known in the gates, where he sits among the elders of the land." Have you ever read this verse in Proverbs 31:23 and not known how it is applicable to you? I like to think of it like this: you, wife, help your husband succeed by appealing to heaven for God's supernatural help in all areas of his life.

As a Godly wife, your obedience to God and submission to your husband, which is directly related to the level of your prayer life, propels your husband's influence. Your prayers are vital to your husband's success: success in business, mind, heart, communication, Godly mission as a husband, and for fulfilling the Great Commission. Do you know the specifics of your husband's responsibilities and work life so that you can take them to Jesus in prayer? It would probably mean the world to your husband if you took the time to ask him what he is dealing with, gave him grace, and took his needs to God in prayer. Appeal to God to help him overcome his problems. Imagine how your husband will feel when he discovers that you not only asked him how you can pray, but that you prepared with the Holy Spirit ahead of time.

Go into your secret place, your prayer closet. Whether it's your car, the laundry room, kitchen sink, or wherever you go, intercede for your husband. Ask the Lord for His vision and His presence. Ask Him to protect your husband on his journey with God. Release the internal need to push your husband towards God. Release your need to tell him where he needs God. Instead, use prayer as your petition for God to move in him.

HER HUSBAND IS

Known in the Gates

WHERE HE SITS

AMONG THE

ELDERS OF THE LAND.

PROVERBS 31:23

LISTEN & WATCH

Micah 6:8
He has told you, O man, what is good; and what does the Lord require of you but to do justice, and to love kindness (mercy), and to walk humbly with your God?

Ephesians 5:25
Husbands, love your wives, as Christ loved the church and gave himself up for her, having cleansed her by the washing of water with the Word, so that he might present the church to himself in splendor, without spot or wrinkle or any such thing, that she might be holy and without blemish.

Matthew 28:19,20
Go, therefore, and make disciples of all nations, baptizing them in the name of the Father and of the Son and of the Holy Spirit, teaching them to observe all that I have commanded you. And behold, I am with you always, to the end of age.

PRAY: *GO INTO THE LAND*

Father, I come before you to bless my husband.

Lead him to be the head of our marriage and family,

as you are his head.

Guide him in patience as he diligently seeks answers through

every responsibility and work problem.

God, You know what He needs and I ask that You

intervene so that immediate and full resolution comes.

Grant him the courage to defeat worry.

Draw him closer to You and surprise him with

miracle-sized provision and straight paths, this day.

May my prayers lift up my husband so that

his honor and respectful name

may glorify God, move mountains,

bring healing when he walks in the room,

and bless everyone he is around.

May he walk humbly, justly, and righteously.

May all that know my husband

be blessed. It's time for the thieving spirits to

pay back in full, plus our

7-fold blessing.

JOURNAL PROMPT

Write a prayer that speaks blessing over your husband.

DAY 41:
SAFE IN FATHER'S ARMS

Woman, you are running now! During this fast, you have bloomed and are a fragrance of glory to God. I am so stinkin' proud of you, and here is my giant, Texas-sized, squishy hug: from me to you. You have successfully created a lifestyle out of prayer. And the journey has just begun.

YOU ARE THE PRAYER WOMAN!!!!!!!

I exhort you in your momentum for more of Jesus. My prayer is that you have become richly blessed with courage, hope, and faith. If you have not seen your miracle yet, it's coming. Pray like you know it. Pray like it is here already. And pray without ceasing. If it comes, it comes in God's timing, whether that is in five minutes from closing this book or in five years. Do NOT ever stop praying in faith.

Use this prayer book to repeat as many times over in your life as you wish; alone, or in small groups, in your church, or inside our sisterhood. Every time, you will be in a different place spiritually: in your marriage and in your heart, so, you will always gain heavenly riches by repeating it. Begin with this:

you are safe in Father's arms right where you are,

you are seen,

you are known,

you are held,

you have purpose.

Come alive in the power of your purpose as a Godly wife who prays! Prayer changes everything!

You know it. You've seen it. You have felt it. Now, rise up and go ignite the sisters in Christ around you, as we link arms to let go and let God!

If you're in need of support, reach out and I'd love to hear your story and pray with you. Your next yes to Him could lead to your next promotion in His Army. Where you are led by Jesus, know, that the place itself might not be safe, but that you are always safe in His arms. He is the epicenter of the storm.

Father doesn't promise us a life as wives to be without struggle, fire, or temptation to act in opposition to the fruit the Spirit, but He does promise that He will be there in the midst, giving a way for you to be held. So, Prayer Woman, rest in the promise that Father's arms are always open wide for your comfort, through it all: in the trials, the loss, the unexpected: He is bigger.

When you can grab a hold of this, then you are safely held inside the power of your purpose as a Prayer Woman. Your prayers will no longer arise in agony, because Father has a way of offering His perspective on our situation, and there is always peace in Him.

What will you decide for your day? Will you choose peace, or will you continue to struggle because you can't let go? Stop getting ahead with plans and putting yourself above God. Stop thinking you will figure your own way through, for God's way through is MUCH better. His cup of love runs over for you! He longs to hold your heart and give you rest, not just at the end when you make it through the season, but right now, in the middle. You are safe in Father's arms.

LISTEN & WATCH

Job 5:11
He sets on high those who are lowly, and those who mourn are lifted to safety.

Matthew 5:5
Blessed are the meek, for they shall inherit the earth.

Psalm 37:11
But the meek shall inherit the land and delight themselves in abundant peace.

Isaiah 40:11
He will tend His flock like a Shepherd; He will gather the lambs in His arms; He will carry them in His bosom, and gently lead those that are with young.

Psalm 17:8
Keep me as the apple of your eye; hide me in the shadow of Your wings.

PRAY: *IN THE MIDDLE, I AM SAFE*

When I can't see safety, I invite Your arms to hold me,

so that in You, my spiritual eyes awaken.

When I am over thinking how to get this pain to stop,

here I am, running into Your presence.

When I try to control my situation, to get relief my way,

I am sorry Father.

Forgive me for idolizing myself.

Forgive me of my lack of trust in You, God.

I come before Your throne

as your humble servant,

daughter of the Most High King,

positioned in promise,

purposed in power,

ready to overcome,

as I find shelter in the safety

of your faithfulness.

Your mercy seat is dripping with Goodness

for my heart and my husband's heart,

so I trust in You,

with the covenant You gave us,

and I promise to keep You first

in all my ways, for all my days.

JOURNAL PROMPT

Three ways you will put Jesus first today.

ABOUT THE AUTHOR

LAURA GANT is a daughter of King Jesus, redeemed, made whole, victorious, and heir of God. While I could tell you when I got saved, baptized, why I became a full-time minister, and add in a whole list of earthly qualifications, education, and acknowledgements, it misses the point. The whole point is **Jesus**! I'm just a saint who is in need of my loving Savior everyday. I believe that when doing deep, inner soul work, our focus needs to be more on Jesus and not on the concern of a person. Jesus Christ authorized, authenticated, appointed, and anointed me for this very work for His Kingdom. He breathed these lessons through my own life, and I obediently translated it into a form that women of the Kingdom can plant for her harvest. There are no better credentials than to get them from the Creator. My hope for you is that you do not listen to the words in this devotional as from a mere human, saved by grace, but that you turn to the Holy Spirit and ask for the ministry of His presence to guide you in between the lines. Leave it not up to self-help, but to the holy conviction of the one true God, Yahweh. Set your eyes upon Jesus, and all of the earthly comparisons, evaluations, and qualifications grow dim in the light of His glory and grace.

www.ingramcontent.com/pod-product-compliance
Lightning Source LLC
Chambersburg PA
CBHW060250150626
46553CB00019BA/1580